SWIFT

W9-BPD-416

Jan. 3 - Jan 11, 2004

Birds of Jamaica

A photographic field guide

AUDREY DOWNER
and
ROBERT SUTTON

Photography
YVES JACQUES REY-MILLET

DISTRIBUTED EXCLUSIVELY BY
NOVELTY TRADING CO. LTD,
53 Hanover Street, Kingston, Jamaica

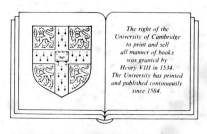

The right of the
University of Cambridge
to print and sell
all manner of books
was granted by
Henry VIII in 1534.
The University has printed
and published continuously
since 1584.

CAMBRIDGE UNIVERSITY PRESS
Cambridge
New York   Port Chester
Melbourne   Sydney

Published by the Press Syndicate of the University of Cambridge
The Pitt Building, Trumpington Street, Cambridge CB2 1RP
40 West 20th Street, New York, NY 10011, USA
10 Stamford Road, Oakleigh, Melbourne 3166, Australia

© Cambridge University Press 1990

First published 1990

Printed in Hong Kong by Wing King Tong

British Library cataloguing in publication data

Downer, Audrey
    Birds of Jamaica.
    1. Jamaica. Birds
    I. Title II. Sutton, Robert L. III Rey-Millet, Yves Jacques
    598.2"97292

Library of Congress Cataloguing-in-Publication Data

Downer, Audrey
    Birds of Jamaica: a complete guide/Audrey Downer and Robert L. Sutton;
    photography, Yves Jacques Rey-Millet
        p.   cm.
    Includes bibliographical references
    ISBN 0–521–38309–9
    1. Birds—Jamaica—Identification. I. Sutton, Robert L.
    II. Title
    QL688.J2D68 1990
    598.297292—dc20 89–77390 CIP

ISBN 0 521 38309 9 Hardcover

GO

For my father Arthur and my wife Ann
R.L.S.

To my children, Richard and Jean,
and grandchildren, Stephen, Natalie and Edward
A.C.D.

To my brother Christian
Y.J.R.-M.

Acknowledgements

Without the help of a great many people this book would have taken many more years to produce. A few people have made an outstanding contribution and our very grateful thanks are due to Catherine Levy for her consistent and dedicated assistance in the field and in the production of this book, and to Andrew Levy for the use of his and Catherine's computer. Patricia Bradley, Desmond Webster and Richard Issa were instrumental in bringing the authors and photographer together and we thank them for their encouragement in the early stages. Ann Sutton critically read the manuscript and made many suggestions for improvement of the text as well as supplying line drawings, maps and some habitat descriptions. David W. Johnston very kindly edited the first draft. Members of the Gosse Bird Club were generous with their observations. We thank the Tenisons of Good Hope, the Williams of Kew Park and the Hawthornes of Shafston, for allowing us to take photographs on their properties. We thank Richard Downer and the staff of Price Waterhouse & Co. who helped with word processing, copying and communications, particularly Heather Lamm and Andrea Chang. The photographer would also like to thank Charles Bornand and Terry Brykczynski for their assistance.

Contents

List of Plates

Front cover: Tody
Back cover: Red-billed Streamertail –
 male

Preface

This book is our answer to all the local and foreign ornithologists, scientists and people with a general interest in natural history who, over the years, have had difficulty identifying some of Jamaica's unique, beautiful and fascinating birds and have requested our assistance. It is a compilation of knowledge gleaned during 25 years of birding, banding and observation (with help from other members of the Gosse Bird Club), and is the first photographic guide to Jamaica's endemic species and subspecies. All species which occur in Jamaica are mentioned, but only endemic species and subspecies, or species that are unique to the Caribbean area, are described in detail.

It is our hope that through this book people will become more aware of and appreciate Jamaica's birds, that they will carry out the research that is needed, take action to protect species that are being affected by hunting and habitat destruction, help others to know and understand them, and simply enjoy a hobby that can last a lifetime, and add a new dimension to travel to foreign countries.

How to use this book

The objective of this book is to facilitate identification of Jamaica's birds in the field. It was decided to concentrate on the birds which are unique to this region, and to complement descriptions of birds which have already been well covered in guides to North American birds. A North American field guide such as *Field Guide to the Birds of North America* (National Geographic Society, 1987), *Birds of North America* (Robbins, Bruun and Zim, 1983) or *A Field Guide to the Birds* (Roger Tory Peterson, 1980) should be used in conjunction with this book.

Scientific, English and local names and systematic arrangement

The classification, nomenclature and systematic arrangement used in this book follow the *Checklist of North American Birds* (American Ornithologists' Union, 6th edition, 1983) with some exceptions to accommodate photographs. The list of subspecies was taken from *A Complete Checklist of Birds of the World* (Howard & Moore, 1980) and *Checklist of Birds of the West Indies* (Bond, 1954 and supplements). There are many local Jamaican bird names, and considerable regional variations in their use exist; thus, only the most widespread and commonly used local names have been listed in the text.

Photographs and descriptions

Photographs are included of all endemic species and most subspecies. Also included are West Indian species which are not illustrated in North American guides. When subspecies are very rare and their present status is unknown (such as Golden Swallow and Plain Pigeon), or when they are pictured in North American field guides (for example Common Ground Dove), they are not illustrated.

All photographs are of wild birds in their natural habitats. It was decided to use photographs because of the importance of posture and surroundings in the identification of birds, and also because of the scientific value of accurate pictures of the rare birds found only in Jamaica. Photographs of some typical habitats are included.

Status

The relative abundance and information as to whether a bird is a resident or migrant is given.

Identification

The 25 endemic Jamaican species, the 21 endemic subspecies and some West Indian and introduced species which are not described in North American field guides have been fully described. This includes details on identification (separate descriptions of the male, female and immature when appropriate), voice, habitat, habits, nesting and range. Notes on identification are based on the authors' observations of wild birds in the field and in the hand. For other species only their status (including dates when they are in Jamaica), voice, differences from similar species, and a summary of range and migration patterns are given. Vagrants are listed in Appendix 1.

Lengths

Only body lengths are given. As far as possible lengths are based on the averages of measurements collected from wild birds in the field by members of the Gosse Bird Club. Measurements (from the tip of the bill to the tail) were taken with the bird held in the hand in as natural a position as possible. Where the Gosse Bird Club had no data, lengths were taken from *Birds of North America* (Robbins *et al.*, 1983).

Voice

The voices of all birds are described (except where vocalisation is so rare that the sounds they make while in Jamaica are not known). Descriptions of voices are based on field observations and a comprehensive collection of tapes. A record of the voices of Jamaican birds is in preparation.

Habitat

The types of habitats used are described for all species. Examples of places where endemic species and subspecies can be seen are pointed out. Vertical migrations are noted.

Habits

Any aspects of behaviour which are useful in identifying a Jamaican species are described. Included are feeding behaviour, main foods, nesting dates, descriptions of nests (where known) and any relevant behaviours.

Range

The range of each species is given to emphasise the incredible journeys some migrants undertake each year between their breeding and wintering areas, or the very restricted areas occupied by other species in the Caribbean region. In the case of Jamaican endemic subspecies, and subspecies that breed in Jamaica with allied races in other areas, the scientific name and the range of the subspecies nesting in Jamaica is given in the first sentence; the next sentence contains the range of the other subspecies.

Parts of a bird

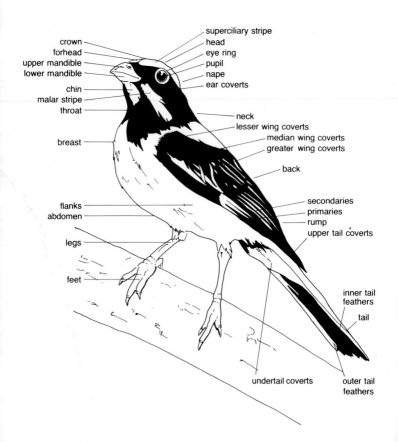

Introduction to Jamaica and Jamaican birds

In Jamaica there are 25 species and 21 subspecies of birds which are found nowhere else on Earth. More endemic bird species occur in Jamaica than on any other Caribbean island or most other oceanic islands around the world. Birding in Jamaica is enhanced by the outstanding beauty of many of the birds, the unique richness and variety of landscape, and the pleasant tropical climate.

General information about Jamaica and Jamaican birds

Location   18° N 77° W; 150 km (95 miles) south of Cuba and 180 km (110 miles) west of Hispaniola; 650 km (400 miles) from Honduras, the nearest mainland. (Fig. 1)

Dimensions   Area 10 982 m^2 (4244 square miles); length 235 km (146 miles); width between 35 km (22 miles) and 82 km (51 miles). Highest point (Blue Mountain Peak) 2290 m (7402 ft). Jamaica is the third largest island in the Caribbean (after Cuba and Hispaniola).

Population   2 355 100 (1987)

Government   Independent British Commonwealth nation since 1962.

Capital   Kingston (Fig. 2)

Language   English (the majority of people speak an English-based dialect).

Climate (Fig. 5)   The climate of Jamaica is tropical maritime. It is modified by the north or northeast trade winds and the daily pattern of land/sea breezes. The average daily temperature ranges between 27 °C (80 °F) in the coastal lowlands to 13 °C (56 °F) in the Blue Mountains. The coolest months are December, January and February. Annual rainfall varies from less than 750 mm (30 in) in the south-central coastal lowlands to more than 7500 mm (300 in) in the John Crow Mountains. The wettest months are usually May and October, but tropical downpours can be expected at any time during the summer months, and 'Northers' sometimes bring wind and rain in winter.

Geomorphology   Jamaica's topography and geology are complicated and diverse, the result of the alternation of periods of volcanic activity and marine submersion. Limestone formations cover more than two-thirds of the island. They include the John Crow Mountains in the east (running approximately northwest–southeast), the east–west ridge of central and

Figure 1   Jamaica and the wider Caribbean

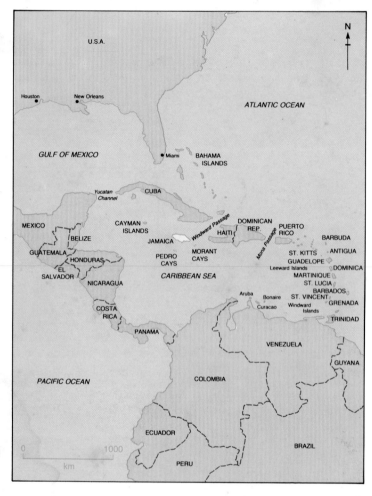

western mountains (including the Dry Harbour Mountains, Cockpit Country and Dolphin Head), the southern coastal hills and two small, north–south ridges in the south-centre (the Don Figureoa and the Santa Cruz Mountains). Between the John Crows and central Jamaica lies the highest range, which is made up of igneous shales, that is the Blue Mountains.

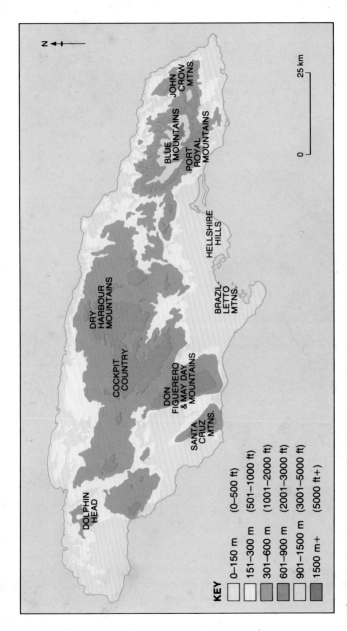

KEY

☐ 0–150 m	(0–500 ft)
☐ 151–300 m	(501–1000 ft)
☐ 301–600 m	(1001–2000 ft)
☐ 601–900 m	(2001–3000 ft)
☐ 901–1500 m	(3001–5000 ft)
☐ 1500 m+	(5000 ft+)

DOLPHIN HEAD

COCKPIT COUNTRY

DRY HARBOUR MOUNTAINS

DON FIGUERERO & MAY DAY MOUNTAINS

SANTA CRUZ MTNS.

BRAZIL-LETTO MTNS.

HELLSHIRE HILLS

BLUE MOUNTAINS

JOHN CROW MTNS.

PORT ROYAL MOUNTAINS

N

0   25 km

Figure 2 Jamaican topography – elevations and main mountain ranges

Some recommended birding areas

There are many beautiful and interesting places to watch birds in Jamaica. This list is not comprehensive but is intended to provide bird watchers with some ideas for places to visit. Listing is alphabetical and numbers refer to Fig.3.

BATH, St Thomas (12)

The Black-billed Streamertail can often be seen in the flowering plants along the road which leads to the historic Bath Fountain Hotel and mineral springs, and in the Bath Botanic Gardens. The gardens were established in 1779 and are the second oldest public **gardens** in existence in the western hemisphere.

BLACK RIVER MORASS, St Elizabeth (40–43)

The largest, most interesting and varied of Jamaica's **wetlands**. Includes the Lower Morass (42) where scenic rivers provide good views of waterbirds. Boat tours can be arranged in Black River. Parottee Ponds (41) are the best place in Jamaica to observe waterbirds, especially waders, in the winter months. Wallywash Pond (40) is sometimes good for freshwater birds. The Upper Morass has been drained for rice cultivation but waders can be observed in the fields at Elim, and Limpkins and Black-crowned Night Herons nest there (43).

CAYMANAS DYKE PONDS, St. Catherine (28)

Located off the Spanish Town to Kingston Highway, a part of the Ferry River has been dammed and the large ponds with reedy edges and rushes provide an excellent habitat for many **wetland** birds. Here the Glossy Ibis, Caribbean Coot and Least Bittern are common particularly in the winter months. Ruddy Ducks, moorhens and coots nest in summer.

COCKPIT COUNTRY (6)

The road from Clark's Town to Albert Town passes through the karst formation of the Cockpit Country. The **wet limestone forest** is spectacular and many endemic species, including the Black-billed and Yellow-billed Parrots and the Jamaican Crow, can be seen. The road is rough and most suited to four-wheel drive vehicles.

CRYSTAL SPRINGS, Buff Bay, Portland (10)

Jamaican Mango and Streamertail hummingbirds are encouraged with syrup feeders, and are numerous, while many other species can be seen in the wild or in cages in the beautiful **garden** which has a natural stream running through it. An entrance fee is charged.

GOOD HOPE, near Falmouth, Trelawny (4)

An eighteenth century sugar plantation, the old greathouse is a private residence and luxury hotel. The birds on Good Hope are less shy than in other areas and this is a good place to see Jamaican Crows and other **wetter limestone forest** species. Twenty of the endemic species can be seen at Good Hope. Bird watchers are admitted by prior arrangement.

GREAT PEDRO POND, near Treasure Beach, St Elizabeth (38)

Large **brackish coastal pond** which is excellent for waders and ducks in winter. Other **small seasonal ponds** in the area harbour Masked Ducks, jacanas, grebes and Yellow-breasted Crake.

HECTOR'S RIVER, Portland (11)

White-tailed Tropicbirds nest in the **cliffs** near Hector's River. The road from Morant Bay to Port Antonio is one of the most scenic drives in Jamaica, and Black-billed Streamertails can be seen in flowering trees and shrubs along the way.

HOPE GARDENS, off Old Hope Road, Kingston (21)

Various species can be seen in captivity in the zoo. There are wild populations of hummingbirds, Yellow-billed Parrots and Night Herons. Migrant warblers are common in the winter. Over 150 species have been recorded in the **gardens**.

MARSHALL'S PEN, near Mandeville, Manchester (37)

Marshall's Pen is a private **cattle property and nature reserve** with extensive tracts of **mid-level limestone forest**. Twenty-three of Jamaica's endemic species are on the checklist for the property. Bird watchers and tours are admitted by prior arrangement. A small contribution is requested.

MONA RESERVOIR and MONA WOODS (22)

Excellent **dry limestone** habitat. A pass is required from the National Water Commission to enter the reservoir area, and permission to bird in the adjoining woods should be obtained from the University of the West Indies, Mona.

MARTHA BRAE ESTUARY, Falmouth (3)

Close to the town of Falmouth, in the estuary of the Martha Brae River, there are marshy areas where **wetland** birds can be found.

NEWCASTLE TO HARDWAR GAP, St Andrew–Portland (23, 24)

The scenic drive through **mature montane forests** provides good opportunities to see many endemic birds. Jamaican Blackbird, Crested Quail Dove, eleanias and pewees are most easily seen here. There are nature trails and picnic areas in the Holywell Forest Reserve.

ROCKLANDS FEEDING STATION, near Anchovy, St James (2)

A private **bird-feeding station** where wild Red-billed Streamertails, Jamaican Mangoes and Black-faced Grassquits come to hand to be fed. Open from 3.00 p.m. to 5.00 p.m. daily. An entrance fee is charged. The surrounding property is **ruinate woodland** and many of Jamaica's endemic species can be observed from the road. It is possible to arrange for a local guide to this area.

PORTLAND RIDGE, Clarendon (30a)

Very arid limestone scrub and the most southerly point in Jamaica. One of the few places where the Bahama Mockingbird can be seen. Pigeons and doves and the Stolid Flycatcher are also common.

YALLAHS SALT PONDS, St Thomas (13)

Natural salt ponds which are good for shore birds and migrant warblers in winter, nesting Least Terns in summer.

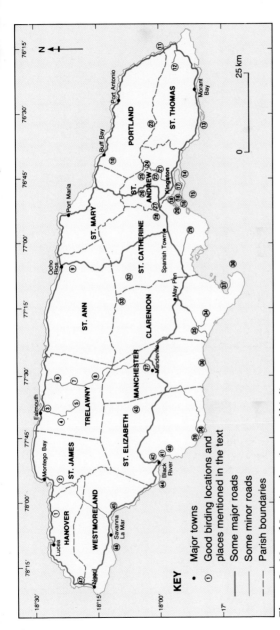

Figure 3 Map of Jamaica showing good birding areas

Key: 1 Tryall Golf Course, Tryall; **2** Rocklands Bird Feeding Station, Anchovy; **3** Martha Brae Estuary, Falmouth; **4** Good Hope; **5** Windsor; **6** Clark's Town; **7** Barbecue Bottom; **8** Albert Town; **9** Fern Gully; **10** Crystal Springs; **11** Hector's River; **12** Bath; **13** Yallahs Salt Ponds; **14** Palisadoes; **15** Port Royal Cays; **16** Port Henderson; **17** Refuge Cay; **18** Kingston Harbour; **19** Hunts Bay; **20** Fort Augusta; **21** Hope Gardens; **22** Mona Reservoir and Mona Woods; **23** Blue Mountain Peak; **24** Newcastle; **25** Hardwar Gap; **26** Stony Hill; **27** Ferry; **28** Caymanas Estate; **29** Salt Island Lagoon, Hellshire; **30** Portland Bight; **30a** Portland Ridge; **30b** Old Harbour Bay; **31** West Harbour; **32** Worthy Park; **32a** Mount Diablo; **33** Mason River; **34** Kemp's Hill; **35** Milk River; **36** Alligator Hole River Project, Canoe Valley; **37** Marshall's Pen; **38** Great Pedro Pond; **39** Treasure Beach; **40** Wallywash Pond; **41** Parottee Ponds; **42** Black River Lower Morass; **43** Elim; **44** Luana or Font Hill, Cave; **45** Pelican Hill, Cave; **46** Cabaritta River, Paradise; **47** Negril Morass, Westmoreland.

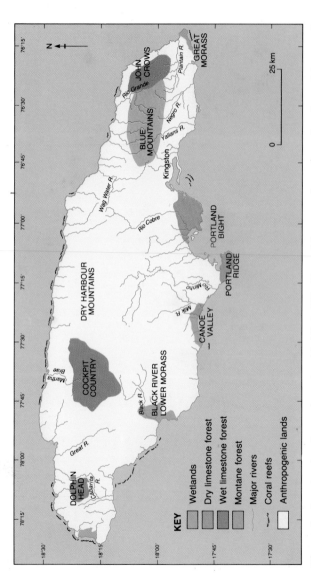

Figure 4 Jamaica showing major natural habitats (NB: Most of the areas shown contain substantial areas of anthropogenic land)

Habitats

From the spectacular coastal wetlands, with their slow, meandering rivers, to the dense wet forests of the mountains with rapid streams and waterfalls, to dry savannas and rolling pastures, there is an astonishing diversity of climate, landscape and vegetation. Jamaica has a very high level of endemism in her natural heritage of plants. At least 784 of more than 3000 species of flowering plants are endemic.

The lowland and riverine forests of Jamaica have been almost entirely cleared since Columbus discovered the island in 1494. The remaining 670 km² (260 square miles) of broadleaf forests can be roughly classified into three main categories; dry limestone (lowland arid) forest found on the southern lowlands and hills; wet and very wet limestone forests of Cockpit Country and John Crow Mountains; and montane forests of the Blue Mountains.

There is also a clear difference between the types and denseness of vegetation on parts of the north and south of the island, produced mainly by the amount of rainfall experienced. As Jamaica is affected by the NE trade winds, the northeastern end of the island, with its high mountain ranges, is the wettest; also, because the central ranges run east–west, the north side is wetter than the south, this has a distinct effect on bird life. Birds such as the Stripe-headed Tanager, Orangequit and White-chinned Thrush are found at sea level in the north, but only in the mountains and foothills in the south. (Fig. 5)

Figure 5 Average rainfall in Jamaica

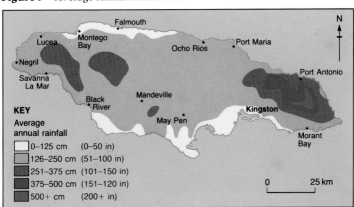

KEY
Average
annual rainfall

☐ 0–125 cm	(0–50 in)
☐ 126–250 cm	(51–100 in)
☐ 251–375 cm	(101–150 in)
☐ 375–500 cm	(151–120 in)
☐ 500+ cm	(200+ in)

Coasts and cays (Plate 1)

Several species of seabirds (including Laughing Gulls, Royal Terns, Brown Pelicans and Magnificent Frigatebirds) are common along the coasts. The small islands around Jamaica (known as cays) support colonies of nesting seabirds, including Sooty Terns and Masked Boobies.

Seabirds are more abundant along the south coast where the broad coastal shelf provides large feeding grounds. On the north coast there is a steep drop-off close to shore and there are spectacular and diverse reefs. The Port Royal Cays and Portland Bight Cays are close to the mainland (Fig. 3). The Morant and Pedro Cays are 65 km (40 miles) and 95 km (60 miles) off-shore. (Fig. 1)

Wetlands (Plates 2 & 3)

Common wetland birds include many species of herons and egrets. Rails, bitterns and tree ducks are present but are secretive and hard to see. Many species of migratory ducks and shorebirds can be seen in coastal ponds and mudflats in winter (e.g. Great Pedro Pond and Parottee Ponds, St Elizabeth, brackish coastal ponds, and Yallahs Pond, St Thomas, a coastal salt pond).

Jamaica's two largest wetlands are the Black River Lower Morass (5700 ha, 14 085 acres) and Negril Morass (2300 ha, 5683 acres). They include mangroves (Plate 2), shallow estuaries, lagoons, salinas, herbaceous swamps (Plate 3) and swamp forests.

Several of Jamaica's wetlands have been unsuccessfully drained for agriculture. Others are threatened by development. Black River Lower Morass (which is very beautiful as well as ecologically important) and Negril Morass could be seriously disturbed if plans to mine their peat reserves as an energy source are implemented.

Plate 1   Morant Cays – offshore cays

Plate 2 Falmouth swamp – mangroves

Plate 3 Salt River, Clarendon – river and herbaceous swamp

Dry limestone forests (Plate 4)

Columbids (including White-crowned Pigeon, Caribbean Dove), parakeets, hummingbirds, Jamaican Woodpeckers, orioles, vireos (especially Jamaican Vireo) and Yellow Warblers, are common all year round in the scrubby growth of this habitat. During the winter, migrant warblers are abundant in dry limestone forests.

Along the coasts, this is one of the most widely distributed habitats. The canopy is usually low (8–12 m high; 20–35 ft), trees are spindly and shrubs are spiny (a few drop their leaves in drought conditions). In cleared, unsheltered areas, tall upright cacti and thatch palms grow in patches. In some places there are many thorny species, such as Logwood and acacias. Thick growths of climbers, vines and strangler figs sometimes make the forest impenetrable, while the loose and bare honeycomb rock make walking precarious. Distinctive trees include Red Birch, Wild Bauhinia (Bullhoof), and agaves (attractive to orioles and hummingbirds). *Broughtonia* and *Oncidium* orchids and bromeliads also occur locally. Dry limestone forest can be seen on the coastal plains and lower hills (such as Dry Harbour Mountains, St Ann). In very dry areas the dry limestone forest is replaced by thorny scrub (for example in coastal Hellshire, south Clarendon and Manchester) (Plate 5).

Plate 4   Portland Ridge, Clarendon – dry limestone forest

Plate 5   Round Hill, Clarendon – dry limestone scrub

Wet limestone forest (Plate 6)

The jabbering calls of Jamaican Crows and the squawking of flocks of parrots overhead are among the unique experiences of birding in this habitat. Yellow-billed and Black-billed Parrots, Jamaican Woodpeckers, Jamaican Todies and Arrow-headed Warblers are common. Rarer birds, such as Ring-tailed Pigeon and the Jamaican Blackbird, can also be seen.

Wet limestone forests occur in the rugged John Crow Mountains, Dolphin Head and the Cockpit Country (for example in Trelawny at Windsor and Good Hope or on the Burnt Hill road, from Clark's Town to Albert Town). The forest is layered and may be as high as 15–20 m (50–65 ft) with occasional examples of West Indian Cedar and Broadleaf reaching 25–35 m (80–115 ft). There is a layer of shrubs and herbs which includes sweetwoods and thatch palms and many vines and bromeliads. The forest floor is dark, with many species of fern growing between outcrops of broken rock. Many plants like Mountain Pride, shrubs and orchids have colourful flowers.

Plate 6 Cockpit Country, Trelawny – wet limestone forest

Montane forests (Plate 7)

The haunting, flute-like calls of the Rufous-throated Solitaire heard echoing across the valleys are characteristic of the Blue Mountains. Other characteristic birds include Crested Quail Dove, White-eyed Thrush and Blue Mountain Vireo. The rare Jamaican Blackbird may be observed foraging for insects in the lush growth of bromeliads and tree ferns.

Hardwar Gap in the Port Royal Mountains above Kingston is the most accessible place to see this type of forest which is restricted to the Blue and upper Port Royal Mountains. The forests are many-layered, lush, dark, dense and cool. There are many large trees which are often heavily overgrown with bromeliads, orchids, creepers and fungi. Long strands of grey lichen trail from their branches.

If the forest is undisturbed, the main canopy is composed of large timber trees like Santa Maria, Blue Mahoe, and a huge variety of other species including Yacca. About 60% of the plant species of the montane forest are endemic. In the sub-canopy there are several species of Sweetwoods, Waxwood, Winterberry and many other smaller tree species. There is a dense and varied shrub layer, with many species which

Plate 7 Blue Mountains, Portland – montane forest

have large beautiful leaves and flowers. Many plants are evergreen and have dark green, waxy leaves with drip-tips which encourage water to run off to the ground. The ground may be covered with mosses and ferns; where a fallen tree creates a break in the canopy, groups of elegant tree ferns may be found. Roadsides are thickly covered with Ginger Lilies which are attractive to hummingbirds. Above 1500 m (5000 ft) the forests are often shrouded in mist for most of the day and the elfin forest is stunted, gnarled and twisted.

The rate of destruction and disturbance of Jamaica's broadleaf forest has been estimated at 20 km² (8 square miles) each year. Sylviculture, coffee planting, illegal cultivation and charcoal burning are some causes of forest loss.

Cultivation (Plates 8 & 9)

More than 75% of Jamaica's land surface is either cultivated or disturbed. Some cultivated areas are good for bird watching. The edges of pastures (Plate 8) and cattle ponds, gardens which include mature trees and mixed cultivation (such as Hope Gardens, Crystal Springs, Good Hope and Marshall's Pen – Plate 9) can be pleasant and productive places to watch birds. Common birds include grassquits, kingbirds, doves, warblers, flycatchers and vireos.

Plate 8   Pantrepant, Trelawny – cattle pasture

Plate 9   Marshall's Pen, Manchester – gardens

Introduction to Jamaican birds

Origin of Jamaica's avifauna

Jamaica's birds are more closely related to the birds of Central America than to those of North or South America. It has been suggested that most West Indian birds are derived from those which inhabited the most southern part of the North American continent before the end of the Tertiary period, when the Panamanian land bridge first joined North and South America. Jamaica has many species in common with Central America. They probably colonised Jamaica during the last ice age, when low sea levels exposed the relatively shallow banks between Honduras and Jamaica. High levels of endemism on Caribbean islands are the result of geographic isolation. Some of the birds which arrived on the islands by chance, evolved into new species. Interestingly, bird species which occur both on the islands and the mainland tend to be more flexible in their habits on the islands.

It is relatively easy to explain the evolutionary relationships of most of Jamaica's endemic species because the majority belong to genera which are distributed throughout the region. However five species (the Jamaican Owl, Streamertail, Orangequit, Jamaican Blackbird and Yellow-shouldered Grassquit) are not obviously closely related to other species in Jamaica or the rest of the world.

Composition of Jamaica's avifauna

Jamaica's avifauna is composed of 200 species and 50+ vagrants or rare winter visitors. The 200 species include 25 endemic species (including 5 endemic genera); 21 endemic subspecies, 4 introduced species, 54 other breeding species, 8 that migrate to Jamaica to breed in the summer and 1 that breeds on the island in winter, making a total of 113 breeding species. There are 74 winter visitors (18 of which increase local breeding populations in winter, and 6 in which some non-breeders sometimes spend the summer). In addition to the 50 vagrants, 25 species are transients or rare winter visitors, making a total of 139 migrants, transients or vagrants.

Endangered and extinct birds

The Jamaican Blackbird is probably the most endangered of Jamaican endemic species. It is rare, and restricted to mature montane and wet limestone forests where it forages in bromeliads. Its habitat is being destroyed for plantations of coffee, Caribbean Pine and illegal cultivation. The Ring-tailed Pigeon is another bird of the forests which may be declining in numbers.

Two endemic subspecies which have become very rare are the Jamaica Golden Swallow and the Plain Pigeon. The Black Rail and the Spotted Rail have both been reported from Jamaica but their breeding has not recently been observed.

The Jamaican Parauque (*Siphonorhis americana*), the Jamaican Black-capped Petrel (*Pterodroma hasitata caribaea*) and the Uniform Crake (Red Rail) (*Amaurolimnas concolor*) are considered extinct.

A birding calendar for Jamaica

The daily and annual patterns of activity of birds in Jamaica are described below.

The best times of day for birding are the early morning and afternoon when birds are most active. Sunrise is between 6 and 7 a.m. in the winter, and 5 and 6 a.m. in the summer (Jamaica uses Eastern Standard Time all year). Sunset is between 5 and 6 p.m. in the winter and 6 and 7 p.m. in the summer. During the heat of the day birds tend to be less active. The afternoon is the best time to observe shorebirds. Night birds are most active at dawn and dusk and at full moon.

December–February
Some local species start to sing and nest. Nesting activity tends to follow rainy periods. Some birds migrate to lower altitudes. Many winter migrants are present.

March
Many local species undergo their pre-nuptial moult and begin to sing. Summer residents arrive and start to sing and nest. Winter migrants also moult into breeding plumage, and northward migration of visitors and transients begins.

April–June
This is the peak of the local breeding season and many species are singing. Flowering trees bloom after or during the May rains. All winter migrants leave by the first week in May.

July–September
The hottest time of the year and the time when birds are least vocal. Many immature birds can be seen. Vocalisations are restricted to location calls. At the end of August the transient winter migrants are moving southward and begin to appear in Jamaica. Summer residents begin to leave.

October–November

Birds look scruffy because the post-juvenal and post-nuptial moults are at their height. Some species are breeding. Winter migrants begin to arrive. Summer residents have gone.

Migration

The number of bird species in Jamaica is almost doubled in the winter by migrants from North America. Some spend the winter and some go farther south. Some join resident populations, so that there are more individuals of these species in the winter. In the spring a few species come to the island and the cays to nest, departing southwards in the autumn.

Migration has fascinated humankind since the beginning of time. Where do birds go when they leave their breeding areas, how do they find their way, and why do some birds migrate while others stay behind? Only in recent years, through placing numbered bands on birds' legs, has the route of flight of many migrants been traced. In North America three or four main corridors have been identified, the two used by most migrants through the West Indies being the Atlantic and the Mississippi 'flyways'.

Bird-banding is done by qualified persons the world over. Birds are banded in the nest, near their regular feeding territory, or are trapped en route to their wintering or breeding areas and a band is placed on one leg. The species band number, date and place of banding is recorded, and the data are sent periodically to a central station; in the case of migrants in Jamaica to the US Fish & Wildlife Service in Washington. When the bird is 'recovered' (killed or found dead) or 'recaptured' (alive and subsequently released), the finder or trapper sends the name of the species (if known) the number of the band, date and place of finding or capture to Washington where the information is entered into a computer; the finder is advised where the bird was banded and when, and the bander is told where 'his' bird was found. Over the years these data have provided information on the ranges of most North American migrants. The band should NEVER be removed from the leg of a live bird because it may be recaptured again somewhere else. In Jamaica, the Gosse Bird Club has a banding permit and carries out regular banding operations. Local birds are banded with the Club's bands and 'recoveries' or 'recaptures' should be reported to the Gosse Bird Club or the authors of this book.

There are two types of migration mentioned herein, altitudinal and longitudinal. Altitudinal migration is demonstrated by such mountain birds as the Solitaire and White-eyed Thrush which, in winter, leave the high mountains and descend to lower elevations where fruit and berries mature earlier. In the summer months many lowland birds go to the higher hills to nest. The migration which is most obvious is the longitudinal. At the end of August new 'chipping sounds' are heard in gardens, and small colourful, new birds appear. These are the Wood Warblers. Many waterbirds appear in swamps and ponds. In spring a few species from South America come to the island to nest, returning south in the autumn. Banding operations have proved that many of these birds return to the very same small garden or area where they had been banded previously and repeat this feat for many years in succession.

How birds find their way with such accuracy has been the subject of many experiments. Some results seem to indicate that birds use celestial navigation as well as surface features and the Earth's magnetic forces to guide them, but this aspect of migration is still largely a mystery. The reason birds migrate, other than in search of food which is scarce or non-existent in northern regions in winter, is in response to hormonal changes and to light and weather changes. As the days get shorter and leaves fall, the insects that depend on leaves for food go into hibernation. Wetlands freeze over. To the south, days are longer, insects and marsh vegetation abound, and pond life is active, so it is natural for birds that depend on this type of food to move south in front of the approaching winter. Coming southwards the pace is leisurely. The birds are tired after a hectic nesting season and they have moulted into their dull non-breeding plumage that blends well with the autumn colours, making them less conspicuous to predators, such as hawks, which are also migrating. When they are faced with an over-water flight in order to reach their wintering grounds, they accumulate a reserve of fat by feeding on which to survive until they reach land and can feed again. The northward migration is usually more hurried. Increasing daylight brings on hormonal changes which enlarge the gonads and increase weight. In some species the adult males leave the wintering grounds before the females and immatures and have established a territory before the latter arrive. Nesting can then start immediately because the time available is short. While in winter quarters, the birds moult into breeding plumage, so that the Black-bellied Plover recovers his black belly and the Spotted Sandpiper his spots; a sombre brown male Indigo Bunting gradually becomes a brilliant blue.

The miracle of bird migration is well demonstrated in Jamaica, and much concern is felt for the resting and feeding areas of these long-distance travellers. The way is hazardous as the migration route and destination points are often drastically altered by natural events and human disturbance. Storms, high buildings and bright lights account for many casualties; the filling-in of swamps and ponds, and the destruction of forests often means a shortage of food so that the birds have to keep moving on, or die.

Legal protection of Jamaican birds

Almost all birds in Jamaica and their eggs are protected under the Wild
Life Protection Act (1974) which prohibits hunting, harassment, capture
and possession of 'the whole or any part' of a protected bird. Excluded
from this provision are game birds in a shooting season and birds which
have been termed pests under the Act. Shooting season dates (if any), bag
limits and other provisions are declared annually by the Minister of
Agriculture. The Wild Life Protection Act is administered by the Natural
Resources Conservation Division. Predation and competition with introduced species, hunting for sport, the pet trade and subsistence (governed
by laws which could be better enforced), and disease are other factors
which affect island birds.

The creation of a well-run system of national parks is urgently needed
to preserve Jamaica's rich heritage of birds and other species. Public
education on the ecological and economic value of birds, law enforce-
ment, revision and consolidation of environmental legislation, the
improvement of the government agencies responsible for the environment, and research are also needed to ensure the future of Jamaica's bird
populations.

History of ornithology in Jamaica

Jamaica's birds were first described by Hans Sloane after he visited
Jamaica in 1687–9. In 1844–6, Philip Henry Gosse came from England to
explore Jamaica's natural history. He made extensive collections and
wrote and illustrated the first books devoted to Jamaica's birds. Extracts
from Gosse's work were recently republished in *Gosse's Jamaica 1844–45*
edited by D. B. Stewart. In 1936 James Bond produced *A Guide to the Birds
of the West Indies* which is still the authority on birds of this region. The
most important recent publication about Jamaica's birds is David Lack's
Island Biology in which his theory of the biogeography of island birds is
described based on the land birds of Jamaica.

Gosse Bird Club

The Gosse Bird Club was founded in 1963 to stimulate the study and
conservation of Jamaican birds. It was named after P. H. Gosse (see
above). Notes and short articles about birds are published in the Gosse
Bird Club *Broadsheet*, which is sent to members twice a year. The Gosse
Bird Club also coordinates Jamaica's bird-banding (ringing) programme.
New members, enquiries and notes and articles for the *Broadsheet* are
always welcomed.

Bird families

Grebes (Podicipedidae)

A cosmopolitan family, two species breed in Jamaica. Duck-like in appearance but with pointed bills, when disturbed they often dive or sink gradually rather than fly, and patter across the water to assist take-off.

Least Grebe *(Tachybaptus dominicus)*
DUCK-AND-TEAL, DIVER   16.5 cm (6.5 in)

Common resident on small ponds, reservoirs and temporary bodies of fresh water.
Nests   Year round.
Voice   Rapid raspy 'tetetetete . . .'.
Range   *T.d.dominicus* Greater Antilles, Bahamas, Central and South America, rare in N. America.

Pied-billed Grebe *(Podilymbus podiceps)*
DUCK-AND-TEAL   23 cm (9 in)

Common resident on ponds, rivers and reservoirs. Adults have pied bills all year.
Nests   Year round.
Voice   A loud 'cow-cow-cow-cow . . .'.
Range   *P.p.antillarum* the Antilles and Central America; also North and South America. In winter local populations are increased by North American migrants.

Tropicbirds (Phaethontidae)

Tern-like birds. In the adults the two central tail feathers are elongated into streamers. Of two species occurring in the West Indies, one comes to Jamaica to nest.

White-tailed Tropicbird *(Phaethon lepturus)*

Bo'sun Bird   66 cm (26 in)

Locally common winter resident (Oct–Jun).
Nests   Jan–Mar, in crevices in coastal cliffs in northeast and southeast.
Most easily seen early or late in day from cliffs in Hector's River or from
sea coast hotels in Ocho Rios.
Voice   A tern-like 'keek-keek'.
Range   *P.l.catesbyi* Antilles, Bahamas and Bermuda. Also pantropical,
pelagic.

Boobies (Sulidae)

A pelagic family, two species of which nest in colonies on the Morant and
Pedro Cays off the mainland. The 'booby eggs' which are a traditional
Jamaican delicacy are actually the eggs of the Sooty Tern and Brown
Noddy. Most seabirds are called 'boobies' in Jamaica.

Masked Booby *(Sula dactylatra)*

Booby   68.5 cm (27 in)

Locally common resident, on cays or at sea.
Nests   Sep–Nov.
Range   *S.d.dactylatra* Bahamas, Pedro and Morant Cays. Also pan-
tropical.

Brown Booby *(Sula leucogaster)*

Booby   58.5 cm (23 in)

Locally common resident, on cays or at sea. Immatures are occasionally
seen on south coastal beaches.
Range   *S.l.leucogaster* West Indies. Also pantropical.

Pelicans (Pelecanidae)

Large diving waterbirds with long, pouched bills which are used to scoop
up fish. They swim buoyantly and often fly in lines, with their heads
drawn back on their shoulders, following the leader's flaps and glides. The
Brown Pelican is the only member of the family that dives for its food.

Brown Pelican *(Pelecanus occidentalis)*
OLD JOE   104 cm (41 in)

Common resident, in coastal waters, on reservoirs, fish farms and in marshy areas.
Nests Dec–Jul in mangroves.
Range *P.o.occidentalis* West Indies. Also coastal North, Central and South America.

Frigatebirds (Fregatidae)

Only one species is found in the northern hemisphere. Large black, or black-and-white seabirds with deeply forked tails, their narrow wings are sharply angled. Often roost with Brown Pelicans.

Magnificent Frigatebird *(Fregata magnificens)*
MAN-O'-WAR BIRD   89 cm (35 in)

Common resident, often seen over fishing beaches where they scavenge waste fish or pirate fish from terns and pelicans.
Nests Dec–Mar in coastal shrubs and trees.
Range *F.m.magnificens* West Indies. Also tropical oceans around the Americas.

Bitterns and Herons (Ardeidae)

A large, cosmopolitan family of long-legged wading birds, usually found in wetlands. They are more numerous in Jamaica in the winter when North American migrants are present. Cattle Egrets spread to the West Indies in the 1950s and were first seen in Jamaica in 1953. Herons and egrets are often called 'gaulin'.

Least Bittern *(Ixobrychus exilis)*
GAULIN   28 cm (11 in)

Locally common resident, shy and inconspicuous in rushes and reeds beside rivers, and in marshes. Told from darker-winged Green-backed

Heron by *smaller size and by rufous wings with buffy wing patches*.
Voice A harsh 'cyak-cyak-cyak-cyak . . .' and soft, fast 'Uh-uh-uh . . .'
Range West Indies and the Americas. Numbers are increased by North American migrants in winter.

Great Blue Heron *(Ardea herodias)*
BLUE GAULIN   96.5 cm (38 in)

Common winter visitor (Jul–May) in wetlands; a few may spend the summer. Larger size and black underparts distinguish this heron from the Tricoloured.
Voice A nasal 'cro-aaark'.
Range North America, wintering in West Indies and Central America south to northern South America.

Great Egret *(Casmerodius albus)*
CRANE   81 cm (32 in)

Common resident seen in wetlands.
Nests Mar–Jun in mangroves.
Voice A snoring 'cro-aak'.
Range *C.a.egretta* Bahamas and Greater Antilles. Also worldwide. Numbers in West Indies, Central and South America are increased by migrants from North America in winter.

Snowy Egret *(Egretta thula)*
WHITE GAULIN, GOLDEN SLIPPERS   51 cm (20 in)

Common resident in wetlands. Distinguished from other white herons and egrets *by golden feet*.
Nests Mar–Jun in mangroves (often in mixed colonies with Cattle Egrets).
Voice A harsh 'aaark'.
Range North America and the West Indies. Local populations are increased by migrants in winter.

Little Blue Heron *(Egretta caerulea)*
BLUE GAULIN   56 cm (22 in)

Common resident. White juvenile told from Snowy Egret by *light-tipped bluish bill and greenish legs*.
Nests Mar–Jun in colonies often with Cattle Egrets.
Range Bahamas, West Indies and the Americas. Local populations are increased by migrants in winter.

Tricoloured Heron *(Egretta tricolor)*
GAULIN 56 cm (22 in)

Fairly common resident in wetlands and ponds island-wide. Distinguished from other blue herons by *white underparts*.
Voice A harsh 'croak'.
Range *E.t.ruficollis* Bahamas, Greater Antilles and the Americas. Local populations are increased by migrants in winter.

Reddish Egret *(Egretta rufescens)*
GAULIN 63.5 cm (25 in)

Uncommon winter visitor in wetlands and saline ponds (Oct–Mar). In white phase (which is most common in Jamaica) *larger size, black legs, feet and bill with bare pink facial skin*, and *active feeding habits* distinguish this species from Snowy Egret and immature little Blue Heron.
Range Coastal southern North America, and Central America. Migrates to the Bahamas and Greater Antilles (rare in Jamaica and Puerto Rico).

Cattle Egret *(Bubulcus ibis)*
TICK BIRD 43 cm (17 in)

Very common resident, in pastures and open areas.
Nests Year round in colonies beside water.
Voice A cackling 'kercuk-oo, kercuk-oo' usually in flight.
Range Worldwide.

Green-backed Heron *(Butorides virescens)*
GAULIN 35.5 cm (14 in)

Common resident on fresh and salt water edges. Immature distinguished from Least Bittern by *dark brown wings*, no wing patches.
Voice A loud 'kwow' or 'cuk-cuk-cuk-ow'.
Range *B.v.maculatus* the Antilles and Central America. Also the Bahamas; North and South America. Northern populations winter south to South America.

Black-crowned Night Heron *(Nycticorax nycticorax)*
QUOK 51 cm (20 in)

Fairly common resident on beaches and in wetlands. Largely nocturnal.
Nests Apr–Aug in trees or rushes.
Voice 'Quok'.
Range *N.n.hoactli* the Antilles. Also worldwide except Australia.

Yellow-crowned Night Heron *(Nycticorax violaceus)*
QUOK, CRAB-CATCHER   53 cm (21 in)

Common resident on beaches and in wetlands. More widespread and less nocturnal than Black-crowned Night Heron.
Nests   Apr–Aug.
Voice   'Quaaark'.
Range   *N.v.bancrofti* West Indies and Central America. Other races in Central and South America.

Ibises and Spoonbills (Threskiornithidae)

Ibises resemble herons but have decurved beaks, and fly with necks and legs extended. Only two of the three species found in the West Indies have been recorded in Jamaica.

White Ibis *(Eudocimus albus)*
CURLEW   56 cm (22 in)

Uncommon resident in mangroves.
Nests   Apr–May in mangroves around Kingston Harbour in mixed colonies with herons and egrets.
Voice   When alarmed, 'hunk, hunk, hunk . . .'.
Range   Greater Antilles (casual in Puerto Rico). Also North and South America.

Glossy Ibis *(Plegadis falcinellus)*
CURLEW   48 cm (19 in)

Rare resident and common winter visitor in flooded fields (off Spanish Town Highway near Ferry) and open marshes (Caymanas).
Nests   A few nest (Apr–May) in mixed colonies with White Ibis.
Voice   'Ka-onk, ka-onk'.
Range   Worldwide.

Flamingoes (Phoenicopteridae)

Flamingoes are large salmon-pink waterbirds with extremely long necks and legs. The thick tricoloured bill is angled downward in the middle, and they feed in a peculiar manner by turning the bill upside down and shifting it back and forth in shallow water as they strain small marine life out of the sand or mud.

Greater Flamingo *(Phoenicopterus ruber)*
FILLYMINGO   106.5 cm (42 in)

Rare winter visitor or transient (Jan–Mar) in coastal ponds, in the sea or on exposed reefs.
Range Yucatan, southern Bahamas and Bonaire. Wanders through Bahamas and Antilles. Also breeds in the Americas.

Ducks (Anatidae)

Ducks usually have broad flat beaks and webbed feet. Only three wild species breed in Jamaica; others are migrants from North America. Like grebes they are collectively known as 'duck-and-teal'.

West Indian Whistling Duck *(Dendrocygna arborea)*
WHISTLER, WHISTLING TEAL, WHISTLING DUCK, MANGROVE DUCK,
WEST INDIAN TREE DUCK, NIGHT DUCK   53.5 cm (21 in)

Status Resident, probably locally common but extremely shy and rarely seen. Numbers have been reduced by illegal shooting.
Identification Bill dark grey. Crown and centre of hind neck black. Back and wings brown, with light edging to feathers. Upper face chestnut, lower face and throat white, neck and breast buff finely streaked with black, becoming broader on abdomen. Flanks black with tear-drop-shaped white spots. Legs long and grey. Tail black.
Voice A shrill five-noted whistle, usually uttered in flight. 'Pi-pi-pee-pee-pee' descending.
Habitat Mangrove swamps at Parottee, Black River Lower Morass, Negril Morass, Falmouth Swamp, Salt Island Lagoon, Grant's Pen, Caymanas Dam.
Habits Largely nocturnal. Leaves roosting sites at dusk for feeding areas in rice, millet and guinea-corn fields, where it arrives after dark. Also eats berries of Royal Palm. Occasionally seen in the day, flying over or standing in swamps, when *goose-like appearance* is diagnostic.
Nests May–Oct in bromeliads, or holes in trees, or in reeds on the ground.
Range Bahamas, Greater Antilles and northern West Indian islands.

Mallard *(Anas platyrhynchos)*
DUCK-AND-TEAL   40.5 cm (16 in)

Uncommon winter visitor and transient (Nov–Jan). Common domesticated duck.
Range   Worldwide.

Green-winged Teal *(Anas crecca)*
TEAL, DUCK-AND-TEAL   26.5 cm (10.5 in)

Rare winter visitor and transient (Nov–Jan) on fresh and brackish ponds.
Range   North America, wintering to the West Indies and northern South America.

Blue-winged Teal *(Anas discors)*
TEAL, DUCK-AND-TEAL   28 cm (11 in)

Common winter visitor and transient (Sep–Mar) on fresh and brackish ponds.
Voice   Peeping notes or (female) very soft quacks.
Range   North America, wintering to West Indies, Central and South America.

Northern Shoveler *(Anas clypeata)*
SPOONBILL   35.5 cm (14 in)

Uncommon winter visitor (Sep–Mar).
Range   North America, wintering to the West Indies and northern South America.

American Wigeon *(Anas americana)*
                                                     35.5 cm (14 in)

Uncommon winter visitor and transient (Nov–Jan) on fresh and brackish ponds.
Range   North America, migrating to northern South America via the West Indies in winter.

Ring-necked Duck *(Aythya collaris)*
                                                     30.5 cm (12 in)

Uncommon winter visitor and transient (Sep–Mar).
Range   North America, wintering to Central America and the West Indies.

Lesser Scaup *(Aythya affinis)*
BLACK DUCK, BLACK HEAD   30.5 cm (12 in)

Uncommon winter visitor and transient (Sep–Mar) on fresh and brackish ponds and bays.
Range   North America, migrating to Central America, northern South America via the West Indies in winter.

Ruddy Duck *(Oxyura jamaicensis)*
DIVING TEAL, RED DIVER   28 cm (11 in)

Locally common resident on fresh and brackish ponds. Female and young distinguished from those of Masked Duck by *single dark stripe across face*.
Nests   Mar–Oct in thick rushes.
Voice   A fast 'kick-ik-ik-ik-ik'.
Range   *O.j.jamaicensis* Greater and Lesser Antilles and some Bahama islands. Also North America. Northern populations migrate to South America via the West Indies in winter.

Masked Duck *(Oxyura dominica)*
SQUAT DUCK, DUCK-AND-TEAL   25 cm (10 in)

Uncommon resident on freshwater ponds fringed with dense aquatic vegetation. Very secretive. Female and young have *two dark stripes across face* (see above).
Nests   Jun–Oct.
Voice   A soft dove-like cooing and a descending 'du-du-du-du-du'.
Range   Greater Antilles. Casual in southern North America, the Bahamas and the Lesser Antilles. Also occurs in Central America south to central South America.

American Vultures (Cathartidae)

The Turkey Vulture is the only resident vulture in the West Indies and the most common large soaring bird in Jamaica.

Turkey Vulture *(Cathartes aura)*
JOHN CROW   63.5 cm (25 in)

Common resident. The head is red in adults and dark in immatures. Nestlings are white, and occasionally partial albinos are seen.

Nests Jan–May on the ground at the base of large trees or under overhanging rocks.
Voice A hoarse hiss (usually at nest).
Range *C.a.aura* Greater Antilles and some islands of the Bahamas. Also North, Central and South America.

Hawks (Accipitridae)

Although there are many species of hawks in the Americas, only the Red-tailed Hawk is resident in Jamaica. The Osprey is a winter visitor and several others are winter transients.

Osprey *(Pandion haliaetus)*
Fish Hawk, Fish Eagle   56 cm (22 in)

Common winter visitor (Sep–May) usually near water.
Voice Sharp, shrill 'cheep'!
Range Worldwide. North American migrants winter to the West Indies and South America. Non-breeders occasionally spend the summer in Jamaica.

Red-tailed Hawk *(Buteo jamaicensis)*
Chicken Hawk   46 cm (18 in)

Common resident.
Nests Mar–May in tall trees at forest edges.
Voice A high, explosive 'chi-uuuuu' descending at the end.
Range *B.j.jamaicensis* Greater Antilles (except Cuba) and northern Lesser Antilles. Also North, Central and South America, the Bahamas and Cuba.

Falcons (Falconidae)

These diurnal birds resemble hawks but have more-pointed wings. Both the American Kestrel and Merlin eat grasshoppers and crickets as well as small vertebrates (such as lizards, frogs, mice and small birds). The Peregrine Falcon feeds on ducks and shorebirds. It is considered an endangered species.

American Kestrel *(Falco sparverius)*
SPARROW HAWK, KILLY-KILLY   21.5 cm (8.5 in)

Very common resident in all habitats.
Nests   Mar–Apr, in holes at the top of dead tree trunks.
Voice   A high-pitched, rapid 'killy-killy-killy' or 'yip-yip'.
Range   *F.s.dominicensis* Jamaica, Hispaniola and adjacent islands. Also Cuba and Isle of Pines; other West Indian islands; North, Central and South America.

Merlin *(Falco columbarius)*
PIGEON HAWK, BIRD HAWK   30.5 cm (12 in)

Common winter visitor (Sep–May).
Range   North America, winters in the West Indies and northern South America.

Peregrine Falcon *(Falco peregrinus)*
DUCK HAWK   38 cm (15 in)

Uncommon winter visitor (Nov–Mar), usually seen near saline mudflats.
Range   Worldwide. North American populations migrate to South America via Central America and the West Indies.

Rails, Gallinules and Coots (Rallidae)

Rails have flattened bodies to enable them to move in dense marsh grasses. Most have bold vertical stripes on their flanks. More often heard than seen. Gallinules and coots swim like ducks, have chicken-like beaks and coloured fleshy shields on their foreheads. When alarmed they usually splash over the water and fly for short distances. The downy young are black. Many of these species are locally known as 'duck-and-teal'.

Black Rail *(Laterallus jamaicensis)*
BLACK CRAKE   11.5 cm (4.5 in)

Rare winter visitor (Sep–Apr).
Voice   'Kick-ee-doo'.
Range   North, Central and South America, Cuba, and formerly Jamaica and Puerto Rico. Migrates in winter to Central and South America and the Greater Antilles.

Clapper Rail *(Rallus longirostris)*
MANGROVE HEN   30.5 cm (12 in)

Uncommon resident in mangrove roots, marsh grasses and rushes.
Nests   Apr–Jun in mangrove roots and rushes.
Voice   A harsh chatter.
Range   *R.l.caribaeus* Greater Antilles and Virgin Islands. Also Central and South America, the Bahamas and other West Indian islands.

Sora *(Porzana carolina)*
                                                          17 cm (6.75 in)

Uncommon winter visitor (Oct–Apr), in both fresh and saline swamps.
Voice   'Keet'.
Range   North America. Migrates through southern North America, Central America and the West Indies to South America in the winter.

Yellow-breasted Crake *(Porzana flaviventer)*
TWOPENNY CHICK   14 cm (5.5 in)

Status   Locally common resident.
Identification   Bill dark olive, paler at the base. Crown black. White superciliary stripe and black eye line. Eye red. Sides of head and neck yellowish grey. Back dark yellowish-brown flecked with white. Wings and tail black. Flanks heavily barred with black. Underparts are white with yellow wash on breast. Feet yellow with very long toes.
Voice   A prolonged high-pitched ascending 'peeeeeeep'.
Habitat   Edges of ponds, streams and wet meadows.
Habits   Difficult to flush, then flies feebly a short distance with legs dangling.
Nests   Apr–Jun.
Range   *P.f.gossii* Jamaica and Cuba. Other races in Hispaniola, Puerto Rico, Central and South America.

Spotted Rail *(Pardirallus maculatus)*
                                                          28 cm (11 in)

Status   Very rare winter visitor. Unreported from Jamaica in the last one hundred years, until April 1977 (upper Black River Morass) and March 1987 (found dead in Mandeville).
Identification   Bill green with red spot at base of lower mandible. Head and neck very dark brown, finely spotted with white. Upper back and breast similar with larger spots. Back feathers and wing coverts are edged with lighter brown. Wings black with light brown edges and a few white

spots. Lower underparts to vent greyish brown. Undertail coverts cinnamon. Flanks and front of thighs dark brown barred with white. Legs red.
Voice 'Tuk-tuk-tuk-tuk', faster at end.
Habitat Dense rushes and grasses.
Habits Secretive and nocturnal.
Range *P.m.inoptatus* Cuba, Dominican Republic formerly Jamaica. Other races in Mexico, Central and South America (including Trinidad and Tobago).

Purple Gallinule *(Porphyrula martinica)*
BLUE-PATE COOT   26.5 cm (10.5 in)

Fairly common resident in fresh and brackish ponds and rivers.
Voice A high-pitched 'pink' (adults), loud whistles (immatures).
Nests Apr–Jul.
Range Greater Antilles, casual in the Bahamas and Lesser Antilles, also North, Central and South America. Jamaican populations are increased by migrants from North America in winter.

Common Moorhen *(Gallinula chloropus)*
COMMON GALLINULE, WATER HEN, RED-SEAL COOT   26.5 cm (10.5 in)

Very common resident on fresh and brackish water.
Voice A variety of harsh, quarrelsome high-pitched notes.
Nests Year round.
Range Worldwide. North American migrants increase local populations in winter.

American Coot *(Fulica americana)*
WHITE SEAL COOT   30.5 cm (12 in)

Fairly common resident on fresh and brackish water. Distinguished from Caribbean Coot by small, brownish-red frontal shield.
Voice A series of low rasping variations of 'Ca-cuk-cuk-cuk-cow-cow's'.
Nests Mar–Jun.
Range *F.a.americana* Greater Antilles, Bahamas, North and Central America. Another race inhabits South America. Jamaican populations are increased by North American migrants in winter.

Caribbean Coot *(Fulica caribaea)*
WHITE SEAL COOT   30.5 cm (12 in)

Uncommon resident on fresh water. Large white frontal shield, sometimes tinged yellow distinguishes this species from American Coot.

Voice   Similar to American Coot, 'c-cuk'.
Nests   Apr–Jun (known to interbreed with American Coot in Jamaica).
Range   Most of West Indies, and northern South America.

Limpkins (Aramidae)

Only one species is in this New World family, which is related to cranes. They feed on water snails, frogs, crabs, crayfish and worms and get their name from their distinctive walk.

Limpkin *(Aramus guarauna)*
CLUCKING HEN   56 cm (22 in)

Locally common resident, in swamps and wet savannas near rivers where there is an abundance of water snails, e.g. Sweet River and Elim.
Voice   A series of wailing 'krau-krau-krau kreow' calls, also shrill screams and clucking.
Nests   Apr–Jun in marsh grasses and sometimes trees. Nest is a platform of dried marsh grasses.
Range   *A.g.pictus* Cuba, Isle of Pines, Jamaica and North America. Other subspecies occur in Hispaniola, Puerto Rico and some Bahama islands. Also Central and South America.

Plovers (Charadriidae)

Plovers are similar to sandpipers but have shorter, stouter bills. They are usually seen on sandy shores, running and stopping abruptly and 'freezing' in mid-step. Two species are resident and several others are winter visitors.

Black-bellied Plover *(Pluvialis squatarola)*
LAPWING   24 cm (9.5 in)

Common winter visitor, on beaches and mudflats. When birds arrive in August they are in breeding plumage; by November the black on their bellies is absent. In March black spots begin to appear on underparts and some birds moult to full breeding plumage before departing in early May.
Voice   A clear whistle 'Tlee-oo-ee'.
Range   Worldwide. Arctic populations winter south to South America. A few non-breeders spend the summer in Jamaica.

Wilson's Plover *(Charadrius wilsonia)*
THICK-BILLED PLOVER   16 cm (6.25 in)

Fairly common resident, on sandy beaches and mudflats. *Large thick bill* distinguishes this bird from Semipalmated Plover.
Voice   A high 'wheet'.
Nests   Apr–Jul on sandy beaches.
Range   *C.w.wilsonia* Greater Antilles, Bahamas, and northern Lesser Antilles. Also North, Central and South America.

Semipalmated Plover *(Charadrius semipalmatus)*
14.5 cm (5.75 in)

Fairly common winter visitor (Aug–Mar) on beaches and mudflats. *Small short bill, yellow legs and voice* distinguish this bird from Wilson's Plover.
Voice   A plaintive 'chewee'.
Range   North America, wintering through Central America and the West Indies to central South America.

Killdeer *(Charadrius vociferus)*
TILDEREE, TELL-TALE, KILLDEE   20 cm (8 in)

Common resident in sandy areas and short grass. *Two breast bands* distinguish this plover from Wilson's and Semipalmated Plovers.
Voice   A shrill 'killdeeeer' and a rising 'deee'.
Nests   May–Jul on grassy edges of ponds, reservoirs, also fields and golf courses.
Range   *C.v.ternominatus* Greater Antilles and Bahamas. Also North America, wintering to northern South America via Bahamas and Greater Antilles.

Stilts (Recurvirostridae)

Outstanding black-and-white shorebirds with long, spindly red legs and loud, yipping alarm calls which put other birds to flight. They perform a distinctive broken leg distraction act when disturbed near nest.

Common Stilt *(Himantopus mexicanus)*
CAP'N LEWIS   33 cm (13 in)

Common resident, in fresh and saline ponds.

Voice   A loud yipping.
Nests   Mar–Jun in marshy ponds.
Range   *H.m.mexicanus* Bahamas, Greater Antilles and northern Lesser Antilles, North, Central and South America. Large flocks of visitors and transients from North America increase Jamaican populations in winter. Other subspecies occur worldwide.

Jacanas (Jacanidae)

Only one genus of this worldwide family occurs in the New World. Their extremely long toes enable them to walk easily on floating vegetation such as waterlilies.

Northern Jacana *(Jacana spinosa)*
RIVER CHINK OR POND COOT   18 cm (7 in)

Common resident in fresh and brackish ponds and rivers. *Bright yellow wings, kept elevated after the bird lands and during displays* are characteristic.
Voice   A noisy cackling.
Nests   Apr–Aug on floating vegetation on ponds and rivers.
Range   *J.s.violacea* Cuba and Isle of Pines, Jamaica and Hispaniola. Other races occur in South America.

Sandpipers and Phalaropes (Scolopacidae)

Sandpipers are usually seen in small flocks on beaches, salinas or mudflats. They are often in immature or winter plumage when they arrive in Jamaica, making them difficult to identify. Non-breeders of several species are occasionally seen in the summer.

Greater Yellowlegs *(Tringa melanoleuca)*
                                                          28 cm (11 in)

Fairly common winter visitor (Aug–Apr) on mudflats. Seen throughout the year (most numerous in Aug–Apr).
Voice   A liquid loud 'tchew-tchew-tchew' repeated.
Range   North America, wintering south to southern South America.

Lesser Yellowlegs *(Tringa flavipes)*

22 cm (8.75 in)

Fairly common winter visitor (Aug–May) on mudflats. Often found with Greater Yellowlegs.
Voice   One to three 'tew' notes.
Range   North America, wintering south to South America.

Solitary Sandpiper *(Tringa solitaria)*

18 cm (7 in)

Rare winter visitor and transient (Aug–May) seen on mudflats and pond edges.
Range   North America wintering via West Indies to South America.

Spotted Sandpiper *(Actitis macularia)*

16 cm (6.25 in)

Fairly common winter visitor and transient (Jul–May) on edges of fresh and saline ponds. Spots on underparts are lost by November. *White superciliary stripe* is diagnostic. Constantly teeters and bows when on the ground, and flies with rapid, stiff wing beats.
Voice   A soft 'peet' or 'peet-weet'.
Range   North America wintering via the West Indies to southern South America.

Willet *(Catoptrophorus semipalmatus)*

33 cm (13 in)

Locally common resident, on mudflats and in shallow mangrove ponds. *Black-and-white pattern on raised wings* characterise this species.
Voice   'Will-will-willet' (in flight) or 'kip-kip' (when alarmed).
Nests   Apr–Jul.
Range   *C.s.semipalmatus* Greater and some Lesser Antilles. North American migrants winter to South America via the West Indies.

Whimbrel *(Numenius phaeopus)*

35.5 cm (14 in)

Uncommon winter visitor (Dec–Apr) on beaches, mudflats and ponds.
Range   The Arctic, wintering along coasts of North and Central America and the West Indies. Also Europe and Asia.

Ruddy Turnstone *(Arenaria interpres)*

18 cm (7 in)

Common winter visitor (Aug–May) on mudflats, beaches and rocky coastlines. Non-breeders occasionally seen in the summer. Breeding plumage is lost by November and not regained until shortly before departure in May.

Range Arctic, wintering south to Chile via the West Indies. Also Europe and Asia.

Sanderling *(Calidris alba)*

16.5 cm (6.5 in)

Common winter visitor (Oct–Mar) often seen following the surf on beaches, in flocks usually in winter plumage.

Range Worldwide.

Semipalmated Sandpiper *(Calidris pusilla)*

13 cm (5 in)

Fairly common winter visitor and transient (Aug–Mar) on mudflats and beaches. *Bill slightly flattened at tip* distinguishes it from other sandpipers.

Voice 'Chit' or 'cheh'.

Range Arctic, wintering south to northern South America via the West Indies.

Western Sandpiper *(Calidris mauri)*

13.5 cm (5.25 in)

Fairly common winter visitor and transient (Aug–Mar). Often seen with Semipalmated and Least Sandpipers on mudflats and beaches. In the field it is almost indistinguishable from Semipalmated Sandpipers in winter plumage, except that *tip of bill is slightly decurved and finer.*

Voice A thin 'jeeet' or 'cheep'.

Range Alaska, wintering in North America and West Indies, south to Peru.

Least Sandpiper *(Calidris minutilla)*

12 cm (4.75 in)

Common winter visitor (Aug–May) on mudflats and beaches. *Yellow legs* distinguish them from Western and Semipalmated Sandpipers.

Voice A thin 'kee-eet'.

Range Northern North America, wintering from North America to South America via the West Indies.

White-rumped Sandpiper *(Calidris fuscicollis)*

19 cm (7.5 in)

Uncommon winter visitor (Nov–May) and spring transient on mudflats.
Range North America wintering throughout South America via Central America and the West Indies.

Pectoral Sandpiper *(Calidris melanotos)*

19 cm (7.5 in)

Uncommon autumn transient (Aug–Nov) on mudflats and flooded rice fields. Has *clearly defined dark bib on breast.*
Voice A throaty 'pruk-pruk' or 'frupp-frupp'.
Range Breeds in the Arctic and winters in southern South America.

Stilt Sandpiper *(Calidris himanotopus)*

18.5 cm (7.25 in)

Uncommon winter visitor (Nov–May) on mudflats.
Range Alaska and Canada. Winters south to central South America, via the West Indies and Central America.

Short-billed Dowitcher *(Limnodromus griseus)*

24 cm (9.5 in)

Fairly common winter visitor and transient (Aug–May) on mudflats. *Perpendicular sewing machine-like feeding pattern* distinguish Dowitchers from other sandpipers.
Voice A sharp and rapid 'tu-tu-tu'.
Range Alaska and Canada, wintering south to Brazil through Central America and the West Indies.

Long-billed Dowitcher *(Limnodromus scolopaceus)*

25 cm (10 in)

Uncommon winter visitor and transient (Aug–May) on mudflats. Very difficult to distinguish from Short-billed Dowitcher.
Voice A high-pitched single 'keek', sometimes repeated.
Range Breeds in northern North America and Eurasia. North American migrants winter in Central America and the Greater Antilles.

Common Snipe *(Gallinago gallinago)*

23 cm (9 in)

Uncommon winter visitor (Oct–Mar) in grassy wet pastures and pond edges.
Voice   Usually silent, but utters a harsh note when flushed.
Range   North America, Europe and Asia. Migrates in the New World through the West Indies and Central America to southern South America.

Gulls and Terns (Laridae)

Eight species breed on cays off the south coast. Only one, the Least Tern, nests on the mainland. All gulls likely to be seen in Jamaica have *square tails*, whereas most terns have *forked tails and more-pointed wings*. Gulls and terns are often seen together flying over fishing beaches and harbours and are collectively called 'boobies' in Jamaica. Commercial collection of the eggs of Sooty Terns and Brown Noddies (known as 'booby eggs') has caused a serious decline in their populations.

Laughing Gull *(Larus atricilla)*

33 cm (13 in)

Common resident, on coasts and in harbours. The only gull likely to be seen during the summer.
Nests   Apr–Aug on cays.
Voice   A harsh 'cheeer-ah' or (when breeding) a rising 'he-he-he-heee'.
Range   Coasts of North America, West Indies, and northern South America.

Ring-billed Gull *(Larus delawarensis)*

40.5 cm (16 in)

Rare winter transient.
Range   Worldwide. North American migrants winter in the Bahamas, Greater Antilles and Central America.

Gull-billed Tern *(Sterna nilotica)*

33 cm (13 in)

Rare winter transient.

Range Worldwide. Breeds in North America, Bahamas and Virgin Islands. Winters through Central America and West Indies to South America.

Caspian Tern *(Sterna caspia)*

51 cm (20 in)

Rare winter transient.
Range Worldwide. Breeds in North America, and winters in southern North America, the West Indies and Central America.

Royal Tern *(Sterna maxima)*

45.5 cm (18 in)

Common resident, along coasts.
Nests Apr–Jun on cays.
Voice A nasal 'zeheit'.
Range Throughout the West Indies, central and southern North America and the coast of West Africa.

Sandwich Tern *(Sterna sandvicensis)*

38 cm (15 in)

Common winter visitor (Oct–Mar) along coasts and coastal ponds. Often seen with Royal Terns.
Range North, Central and northern South America, the British Isles and Europe. North American populations winter in the West Indies, Central and South America.

Roseate Tern *(Sterna dougallii)*

38 cm (15 in)

Rare resident. Formerly nested on Port Royal Cays.
Range Worldwide.

Least Tern *(Sterna antillarum)*

21.5 cm (8.5 in)

Common summer resident, nesting on salt ponds and beaches.
Nests Apr–Aug.
Voice A high-pitched 'cheereep' and a short 'kip, kip'.
Range Worldwide. Breeds in Central America, Bahamas, and Caribbean islands. Winters from Central America southwards.

Bridled Tern *(Sterna anaethetus)*

35.5 cm (14 in)

Uncommon summer resident (Apr–Aug) at cays.
Voice   A high-pitched 'erk'.
Range   Dry Tortugas, West Indian islands, Bahamas, northern Central America and West African coast.

Sooty Tern *(Sterna fuscata)*

40.5 cm (16 in)

Common summer resident (on breeding grounds only) at cays or in open waters.
Voice   A nasal 'wideawake' or 'wacky-wack'.
Nests   Apr–Aug on Pedro and Morant Cays.
Range   Pantropical (largely pelagic after breeding season).

Black Tern *(Chlidonias niger)*

23 cm (9 in)

Common summer visitor (Jun–Nov) over rivers and brackish ponds.
Voice   'Kik, keek'.
Range   North America, wintering from Panama south to Chile via the West Indies. Also Old World.

Brown Noddy *(Anous stolidus)*

38 cm (15 in)

Common summer resident (on breeding grounds only), seen at cays or in open waters, nearer to shore than Sooty Terns, or in mixed feeding flocks.
Voice   A growling 'karrrrk' or dry 'kak'.
Nests   Apr–Aug on Morant and Pedro Cays.
Range   Pantropical.

Pigeons and Doves (Columbidae)

The pigeons and doves are a cosmopolitan family of plump birds with small heads. Twelve species are found in Jamaica including two endemic species, three endemic subspecies, and two introduced species which sometimes breed in the wild. Hunting of columbids is a popular sport in Jamaica. A hunting season may be declared annually (Aug–Oct) under the Wild Life Protection Act. Several species are declining as a result of illegal hunting.

Plain Pigeon *(Columba inornata)*
BLUE PIGEON   40.5 cm (16 in)

Status   Very rare and endangered resident.
Identification   A large robust pigeon. Head and breast brownish-crimson with a patch of crimson in median wing coverts. Greater wing coverts edged white forming a *white border to folded wing and a white bar in wing in flight.* Wings light brown. Upper back dark drab, lower back and tail grey: *no white in tail.* Bill light grey; eye white, eye ring red. Abdomen and undertail coverts grey with darker tips. Legs crimson.
Voice   Similar to White-crowned Pigeon, but shorter and higher in pitch: 'cruuuu cru cru'.
Habitat   Open wooded areas in the mountains: Fern Gully, Barbecue Bottom; coastal areas: Yallahs, Clarendon Plains.
Habits   Nests in wet limestone forest (Apr–Jul). Feeds in coastal mangroves, chiefly in southern coastal plains (Oct–Apr).
Range   Jamaica *C.i. exigua* is an endemic subspecies. Rare and local in Cuba but still common in Hispaniola.

White-crowned Pigeon *(Columba leucocephala)*
BALDPATE, BALL PLATE   28 cm (11 in)

Common resident.
Nests   May–Sep in well-wooded areas, in mangroves and Logwood near the coast, and in tall trees in the mountains. Feeds on berries of Red Birch, Pimento, Bullet, Burnwood, Mangrove, peppers and other fruit. Flocks sometimes seen feeding near the coast and flying inland at dusk. Single birds and pairs are found throughout the island.
Voice   A deep 'Who? Who took two? Who took two? Who took two?' Also a purring cruuuuuuuuu.
Range   Breeds in the Florida Keys, Bahamas, and islands of the Caribbean Sea and said to wander among the islands.

Ring-tailed Pigeon *(Columba caribaea)*
RINGTAIL   40.5 cm (16 in)   Plate 10

Status   Resident, fairly common locally, but illegal hunting year-round and destruction of forest threatens its survival.
Identification   A large, sleek light-grey pigeon with a *black band across the middle of the buffy-ash tail* and an iridescent bluish-green patch on the

hind neck. Eye and eye ring red, bill black, throat white, underparts pinkish brown or lavender fading to buffy undertail coverts. Legs red.

Voice   Fairly low-pitched 'cru cru crooooo', last note longer and lower.

Habitat   Forested mountain areas, Cockpit Country, Blue Mountains and John Crow Mountains. Descends to lower elevations in winter.

Habits   Arboreal, rarely seen on ground. Usually found in flocks of 6–20 feeding silently on berries. Incautious and can be approached quite closely. Nests in deep forest in mid-canopy.

Range   Jamaica. An endemic species.

Plate 10   Ring-tailed Pigeon

White-winged Dove *(Zenaida asiatica)*
WHITE-WING, LAPWING   25.5 cm (10 in)

Very common resident in rather arid regions, often near water. Also common in cultivated fields, gardens and in mangroves. Only seen in the mountains in mid-summer. Distinguished from Zenaida Dove by *large white patch on wing*. In flight wings appear to miss a beat.

Voice 'Two bits for two'. The song is more varied than other doves.

Range *Z.a.asiatica* Greater Antilles and western Caribbean islands, and the Bahamas. Also North, Central and South America.

Zenaida Dove *(Zenaida aurita)*
PEA DOVE   28 cm (11 in)

Common resident from sea level to the mountains in wooded cultivations and gardens. Usually seen walking in pairs on paths, roadways or lawns. Wings 'creak' in flight.

Nests May–Jun at the base of coconut fronds or in bromeliads. Differs from White-winged Dove by *dark spots on wings, and white on trailing edge of wing*. Both have white-tipped tails.

Voice 'What AM I to do?' often followed by 'oo-Ah-oo'.

Range *Z.a.zenaida* Bahamas and Greater Antilles. Also Yucatan and offshore islands; Lesser Antilles.

Mourning Dove *(Zenaida macroura)*
LONG-TAIL PEA DOVE, PALOMA   26.5 cm (10.5 in)

Locally common resident in dry, south coastal limestone scrub near water. The *long diamond-shaped tail tipped with white* is diagnostic in flight.

Voice Similar to Zenaida Dove but higher.

Range *Z.m.macroura* Greater Antilles and Central America. Also North America and the Bahamas.

Common Ground Dove *(Columbina passerina)*
GROUND DOVE   14 cm (5.5 in)

Status Very common and widespread resident.

Identification *Male* A small plump dove, grey above with centre of crown brown. Eye red. Bill orange, tipped black. Underparts pinkish brown edged darker on breast, giving a scaly effect. Wings dark rufous, edged dark grey; wing coverts pinkish brown with purple-blue spots. Tail black. Feet vinaceous. *Female and immature* lack the pinkish brown underparts, and are greyish brown.

Voice 'Hoe-Ah, Hoe-Ah, Hoe-Ah', 'Woop, Woop' and other short, repeated calls.

Habitat Dry limestone forest edges and clearings, in the plains and foothills, but less common in the mountains.

Habits Pairs or small family parties are often seen walking on roads or paths from which they fly onwards for a short distance when disturbed. Nests year-round, but chiefly Apr–Jun, in shrubbery near the ground and sometimes in trees.

Range Jamaica. *C.p.jamaicensis* is an endemic subspecies. Other sub-species are found in Bermuda and the Bahamas; throughout the West Indies; North, Central and South America.

Caribbean Dove *(Leptotila jamaicensis)*
WHITE-BELLY   30.5 cm (12 in)   Plate 11

Status Locally common resident.

Identification *Forehead and underparts white.* Head grey becoming glossy rosy-vinaceous on hind neck and collar. Rest of upper parts dark olive, with outer tail feathers lightly tipped white. Face powder-grey, eye beige, bare skin around eye pinkish, bill black. Underwing cinnamon, feet crimson.

Voice A plaintive 'Who cooks for you?', 'What's that to you?'

Habitat Dry limestone forest, but more common in secondary forest with thick tree-cover in the foot-hills, gardens and orchards.

Habits A terrestrial dove, usually seen singly emerging from under-brush, pumping head forward and flicking tail up. It feeds on seeds of fallen fruit such as Orange, Naseberry, and Red Birch, as well as small snails. Nests in Logwood trees or in low bushes.

Range Jamaica. *L.j.jamaicensis* is an endemic subspecies. Introduced on New Providence. Other subspecies inhabit Grand Cayman and St Andrew's Island.

Ruddy Quail Dove *(Geotrygon montana)*
PARTRIDGE   25.5 cm (10 in)

Locally common but difficult to see, on the ground or in dense vegetation, in humid mountain forests and citrus orchards. Descends to lower elevations in winter months.

Nests Apr–Jun in thick shrubbery.

Voice A booming, low moaning 'OOOah, OOOah' repeated for long periods.

Range *G.m.montana* Greater Antilles and Grenada. Also Central and South America; Lesser Antilles.

Plate 11 Caribbean Dove

Crested Quail Dove *(Geotrygon versicolor)*
Mountain Witch, Blue Dove, Blue Partridge   30.5 cm (12 in)   Plate 12

Status   Fairly common resident locally. More abundant in wet years.

Identification   A stocky grey and rufous dove, the grey head feathers elongated and ending abruptly at base of head. *Primaries, upper back and wing coverts rufous and magenta*, lower back iridescent greenish-black. Forehead black, eye and eye ring red, malar patch and chin buffy, bill reddish black. Collar, neck and breast grey, washed magenta. *Lower underparts to tail coverts bright rufous.* Legs red. *Immatures* have browner underparts.

Voice   A two or three-noted 'Woof-woo', first note explosive, last note descending.

Habitat   Undergrowth in wet limestone and montane forest.

Habits   Often encountered walking on country roads and mountain paths, usually in pairs, and after rain. *Pumps head back and forth while flicking tail up and down.* In breeding season (Mar–Jun) often seen on Newcastle/Hardwar Gap road early in the morning. Nests close to the ground. When flushed, does not fly far and may be found nearby in undergrowth. Wings make a whooshing sound.

Range   Jamaica. An endemic species.

Plate 12   Crested Quail Dove

Parrots and allies (Psittacidae)

Parrots and parakeets belong to a large, widespread, mostly tropical family. Representatives of the two native West Indian genera, *Amazona* and *Aratinga*, are both found in Jamaica. Only one other island in the Caribbean (Dominica) has two endemic species of parrot. The Green-rumped Parrotlet is an introduced species from South America.

Olive-throated Parakeet *(Aratinga nana)*
PARAKEET   30.5 cm (12 in)   Plate 13

Status   Common and widespread resident.
Identification   Head, back and long pointed tail green. Eye orange with bare skin around eye cream. Bill pale horn colour. *Throat to abdomen dark olive-brown.* Wings black and blue. Readily distinguished from the Yellow-billed Parrot by *long tail and slender body.*
Voice   A shrill 'creek, creek' in flight or a single 'preeeit', not unlike the Jamaican Woodpecker.
Habitat   Widespread in wooded hills, mountain slopes at lower elevations, scrub in humid or semi-arid areas, cultivations and gardens.
Habits   Nests in termite nests or holes in trees. Generally seen in flocks of 2–20. Eats buds and fruit of many trees, e.g. *Ficus* sp., Red Birch, *Erythrina, Spathodea,* also cultivated crops, often becoming a pest.
Range   Jamaica. *A.n.nana* is an endemic subspecies sometimes regarded as an endemic species, *A. nana* – Jamaican Parakeet. Another subspecies occurs in Central America.

Plate 13   Olive-throated Parakeet

Green-rumped Parrotlet *(Forpus passerinus)*
GUIANA PARROLET, 'PARROLET', PARAKEET   13 cm (5 in)   Plate 14

Status   Common and widespread resident.
Identification   *A tiny green parakeet with a short pointed tail.* Wings black with green wing coverts. Adult *males* have a blue patch in the wings and a blue rump, *females* are yellower on breast. Bill horn-coloured, legs pinky-grey.
Voice   A loud chattering when flock settles in a tree: 'swee-swee-swee-sweetie'. Flight song 'phil-ip, phil-ip, phil-ip'.
Habitat   Widespread at all elevations.
Habits   Usually in noisy flocks. Nests in holes in trees, old woodpecker holes, and eaves of houses. Feeds on Coconut blossom, Indian Corn, Orange, Logwood, *Ficus* sp., grass seed, fruit and small berries.
Range   Introduced into Jamaica in 1918, and Barbados, from South America.

Yellow-billed Parrot *(Amazona collaria)*
PARROT   26.5 cm (10.5 in)   Plate 15

Status   More common resident than the Black-billed Parrot. Threatened by illegal hunting, collecting for the pet trade and habitat destruction.
Identification   *Yellow bill*, paler at tip, is conspicuous in flight. Eye dark hazel; bare skin around eye cream. *Narrow white band on forehead*, head green with blue wash, hind neck feathers deep rose-colour edged with dark grey (giving a scaly effect). *Throat and neck pinkish* edged with green. Rest of body green; lower back and short tail greenish-yellow, base of tail rosy. Wings dark grey, leading edge blue. *Legs yellow*. Wing-beats are shallow.
Voice   A high pitched 'ah-ah-Eeeeek' rising on last note, and 'whip-whip-whip-Waaaark' in flight, also many other squawking noises.
Habitat   Forested limestone hills and mountains. Cockpit Country, Mt Diablo, John Crow Mountains, but rare in the Blue Mountains. A small flock which ranges over St Andrew and St Catherine has become established at Hope Gardens.
Habits   Often seen in pairs or small flocks. Nests in holes in trees or rock crevices. Feeds on seeds and fruit of many wild and cultivated plants, also leaf buds.
Range   Jamaica. An endemic species.

Plate 14   Green-rumped Parrotlet

Plate 15   Yellow-billed Parrot

Black-billed Parrot *(Amazona agilis)*

PARROT   25.5 cm (10 in)   Plate 16

Status   Not as common as the Yellow-billed Parrot, and similarly threatened.

Identification   A plain green parrot. Noticeably smaller and bluer-green than the Yellow-billed Parrot. *Bill dark grey*, lighter at base. Eye hazel, bare skin around eye black. Ear coverts narrowly edged black. Hind neck feathers edged with dark grey giving a scaly effect. Primaries black, leading edge blue, *a few red feathers in greater wing coverts of adults.* Tail short, green; base red, inner web edged with yellow. *Legs dark grey.*

Voice   Similar to Yellow-billed Parrot, but tones are richer and more varied.

Habits   Similar to Yellow-billed Parrot.

Range   Jamaica. An endemic species.

Cuckoos and Anis (Cuculidae)

The cuckoo family is found in both the Old and New Worlds. Five species are found in Jamaica including four residents and a summer migrant. Unlike some Old World cuckoos they do not lay their eggs in other birds' nests.

Mangrove Cuckoo *(Coccyzus minor)*

RAINBIRD   28 cm (11 in)   Plate 17

Status   Common resident.

Identification   Upper parts dark brownish-grey with a broad dark eyeline. Bill decurved, black above, yellow below. Underparts light cinnamon. Tail tipped whitish on outer feathers. *No rufous in wing. Immature* has grey breast and cinnamon lower underparts.

Habitat   Found in low and mid-level dry limestone forest, south coast swamps, orchards and gardens.

Habits   Nests Mar-Jun in shrubbery at low elevations.

Voice   Sometimes a short 'kar-kar-kar', but usually longer and ending 'ca-ca-co-co-coa'.

Range   Jamaica. *C.m.nesiotes* is an endemic subspecies. Also other West Indian islands; North, Central and South America.

Plate 16 Black-billed Parrot

Plate 17 Mangrove Cuckoo

Yellow-billed Cuckoo *(Coccyzus americanus)*
RAINBIRD, MAY BIRD   28 cm (11 in)

Uncommon transient and rare summer resident (Feb–Nov) in lowland dry scrub, e.g. Port Henderson, Hellshire, Milk River, Portland Ridge, Treasure Beach. Rufous outer flight feathers distinguish it from Mangrove Cuckoo.
Nests   (Very rarely in Jamaica) in mangrove and Cashaw trees, in May.
Range   North and Central America, the Bahamas and Greater Antilles, wintering in South America.

Smooth-billed Ani *(Crotophaga ani)*
TICK BIRD, SAVANNA BLACKBIRD   34.5 cm (13.5 in)

Common resident in cultivated land, pastures, and wet meadows.
Nests   Year-round in communal nests in mangroves, bamboo or over-grown creepers, such as *Bougainvillea*, from sea level to the mountains. Eats insects, lizards, nestlings of other birds and some fruit, e.g. Fiddle-wood, Pudding Withe, Orange.
Voice   A high-pitched 'quee-eeek' rising, also growls and clucks.
Range   Most Caribbean islands except Barbados, North, Central and South America.

Jamaican Lizard Cuckoo *(Saurothera vetula)*
OLD WOMAN BIRD, RAIN BIRD, MAY BIRD   38 cm (15 in)   Plate 18

Status   Resident, less common than the Chestnut-bellied Cuckoo.
Identification   Smaller than the Chestnut-bellied Cuckoo and with larger white tips to the graduated tail. Upper half of head dark reddish brown. *Bill straight*, upper mandible dark grey, lower mandible light grey with dark tip. Eye hazel with red orbital skin. Back and central tail feathers light grey, other tail feathers dark grey, graduated and all broadly tipped with white. Throat grey with white centre. Breast to vent yellow ochre fading gradually to cream at tip of undertail coverts. Wings short, ending at rump. *Primary wing feathers and some secondaries rufous*, tipped grey; others grey. Legs light grey.
Voice   Rapid, low, trailing 'cak-cak-cak-ka-ka-ka-k-k'.
Habitat   Widespread in wooded areas.
Habits   Similar to Chestnut-bellied Cuckoo but found lower in trees and shrubs. Often perches with head lower than feet. Nests Mar–Jun in wet mountain areas: Hardwar Gap, John Crow Mountains, Mandeville, as well as in the Cockpit Country. Nest a shallow saucer of criss-crossed twigs lined with leaves, placed in a tangle of branches, twigs and bromeliads. Feeds on lizards, caterpillars, locusts and nestlings of other birds.
Range   Jamaica, an endemic species.

Plate 18 Jamaican Lizard Cuckoo

Chestnut-bellied Cuckoo *(Hyetornis pluvialis)*

OLD MAN BIRD, MAY BIRD, RAIN BIRD   48 cm (19 in)   Plate 19

Status   Common resident.

Identification   *A large grey cuckoo with deep chestnut lower underparts.* The graduated feathers of the long grey tail end in large white spots. Throat cream, breast pale grey. *Dark grey bill slightly decurved,* lower mandible creamy in centre. Legs dark grey.

Voice   Usually heard in April, May and June. The hoarse 'quak-quak-ak-ak-ak-ak-ak', slow at first and accelerating towards the end, is often the first indication of the presence of this bird.

Habitat   Woodland, wooded cultivation, or open thicket and gardens in the hills and mountains. Descends to lower elevations in winter months.

Habits   Runs along the branches like a large rat and glides on extended wings from one tree to another. Eats lizards, mice, insects, caterpillars, nestlings and eggs. Other birds often mob it. Nest (Mar–Jun) in top of tall trees is made of sticks.

Range   Jamaica, an endemic species.

Plate 19   Chestnut-bellied Cuckoo

Barn Owls (Tytonidae) and Owls (Strigidae)

Two families of these nocturnal birds are resident in Jamaica. The endemic Jamaican Owl belongs to a monotypic genus. Unfortunately owls are often killed by superstitious people who believe they are a sign of death.

Common Barn Owl *(Tyto alba)*

SCREECH OWL, PATOO, SCRITCH OWL, WHITE OWL   35.5 cm (14 in)

Common resident. Found from sea-level to the mountains in open or partly open situations, often near human habitations; commonly seen flying over cane fields at dusk or perched on fenceposts by the roadside. Feeds on rats and mice.

Nests Dec–Jul in caves, abandoned buildings, tree cavities.

Voice 'Creek, creek, creek' and a harsh shriek which is supposed to sound like 'the tearing of the shroud!'

Range *T.a.furcata* Cuba, Isle of Pines, Jamaica. Rare in Cayman Islands. Also worldwide.

Jamaican Owl *(Pseudoscops grammicus)*

BROWN OWL, PATOO   30.5 cm (12 in)   Plate 20

Status Common and widespread resident.

Identification A *small tawny brown owl* with dark brown and black flecks in centre of each feather. Back darker; wings and tail barred and mottled with black. Bill light bluish-grey. *Feathers on crown elongated into earlike tufts.* Large, protruding eye hazel; often has blue nictating membrane drawn across eye in day time. Legs and feet tawny.

Voice A hoarse, throaty 'whow', sometimes 'to-whoo', usually heard at dusk and just before dawn. *Immatures* a high 'wheee-eee'.

Habitat Widespread at all elevations, at forest edges, often found in gardens near houses and in open spaces with isolated trees.

Habits Nests Mar–Oct in holes in trees, under bromeliads or in overgrown *Bougainvillea* vines on trees. Feeds on insects, mice, lizards and tree frogs. Often uses the same daytime perch for months at a time.

Range Jamaica, an endemic genus and species.

Plate 20 Jamaican Owl

Nightjars (Caprimulgidae)

Nightjars are a widespread family of nocturnal insectivores which feed chiefly at dusk. During the day they roost lengthways on branches or on nests on the ground. Two species occur in Jamaica, one in summer and one in winter.

Antillean Nighthawk *(Chordeiles gundlachii)*
GIMME-ME-BIT   23 cm (9 in)

Common summer resident (Mar–Sep) in open areas, nesting on beaches, flat rooftops, in bauxite mines, on pine needles and many other stony and grassy areas. Usually seen at dusk, but sometimes seen flying and calling in the day. Distinguished from swallows by larger size and *white band across wing. Males have white in tail.*
Voice   'Gimme-me-bit'.
Range   Greater Antilles, the Bahamas and the Florida Keys. Winters in South America.

Chuck-Will's-Widow *(Caprimulgus carolinensis)*
                                                              28 cm (11 in)

Uncommon but regular winter visitor (Oct–Mar) in low and mid-level woodland, e.g. Kemp's Hill, Mandeville, Malvern, Montego Bay coastal hills.
Voice   Usually silent. Prior to departure in March sometimes calls 'Will's widow'.
Range   North America. Winters from Texas to northern South America via Central America and the West Indies.

Potoos (Nyctibiidae)

Potoos are nocturnal birds which take their prey like flycatchers, by flying out from a perch and returning to the same or a nearby spot. In this they differ from the related nightjars. Potoos belong to a small tropical American family. Only one species is found in Jamaica. Potoos, like owls, are often killed by people who consider them bad omens.

Common Potoo *(Nyctibius griseus)*
<small>PATOO</small>   40.5 cm (16 in)   Plate 21

Status   Locally common resident.

Identification   General colouration of *adults* is dark brown and cinnamon, streaked and mottled with cream. Central shafts of feathers dark brown. Wings and tail very long irregularly barred with greyish cream and dark brown. Bill black, small and hooked. Gape is enormous. Eye yellow, reflects red in light at night. *Immature* plumage white with black feather shafts.

Voice   'Qwaa-a-a-a-a, qwa-qwa-qwa-qwa', also 'wow'.

Habitat   Wooded areas bordered by open clearings with scattered trees. Often found with cattle, on golf courses, in trees on open lots in towns.

Habits   Nocturnal. Uses the same roost and perch regularly for months. Nests Feb–Nov. Lays a single egg on a broken limb or branch and both parents incubate and feed the young. Sits upright on perch with eyes closed. If disturbed it will not flush but may turn or raise head imperceptibly, opening eyes slightly. Feeds on large moths and beetles. Differs from mainland species in that it does not perch with beak held vertically above body, and has a different voice.

Range   Jamaica. *N.g.jamaicensis* is an endemic subspecies. Another subspecies occurs in Hispaniola and Gonave Island. Also Mexico, Central and South America including Trinidad.

Swifts (Apodidae)

Swifts are aerial insectivores similar in flight to swallows with which they often feed, but they are more closely related to hummingbirds. Their wings are swept back in a smooth arc, and they often fly with wings held stiffly below body. Three species nest in Jamaica.

Black Swift *(Cypseloides niger)*
<small>BLACK SWALLOW, RAINBIRD, SWALLOW</small>   18 cm (7 in)

Common resident. Nests in clefts in steep rock faces in the mountains near waterfalls. Often seen with Collared Swifts when *smaller size, lack of white collar and more flapping flight* identify it. Usually seen early in the morning or in the evening at Mona Dam, in Blue Mountains. Uncommon in the west of Jamaica.

Voice   'Tsip-tsip'.

Range   *C.n.niger* Greater Antilles. Also North, Central and South America.

Plate 21   Common Potoo

White-collared Swift *(Streptoprocne zonaris)*
RAINBIRD, RINGED GOWRIE, COLLARED SWIFT   21.5 cm (8.5 in)

Common resident in montane forest and interior valleys. Descends to the lowlands on cloudy days. Nests (May–Jun) are similar to the Black Swift. Flight alternates between flaps and glides.

Voice   A loud shrill 'wee-eet, wee-eet' heard even when the flock is too high to be seen with the naked eye, but often silent.

Range   *S.z.pallidifrons* Cuba, Hispaniola and Jamaica. Also Central and South America including Trinidad and the Lesser Antilles.

Antillean Palm Swift *(Tachornis phoenicobia)*
PALM SWIFT, SWALLOW   10 cm (4 in)   Plate 22

Status Very common resident.

Identification   A very active small swift, black above with a *conspicuous white rump*, underparts white, sides under wing black, meeting in a narrow band across chest in adults. Undertail coverts black. *Immatures* are buffy below. Beak very tiny and black with a wide gape. Tail forked.

Voice   Twittering.

Habitat   Lowlands, common near human habitations, over golf courses, dry swamps and canefields. In hot weather also found in the mountains.

Habits   Nests year-round in colonies in the dead fronds hanging from Thatch Palms. Flight batlike, alternating between rapid wing beats and gliding, wheeling, diving and twisting from side to side.

Range   *T.p.phoenicobia* Jamaica, and Hispaniola and adjacent small islands. Another race inhabits Cuba.

Plate 22   Antillean Palm Swift

Hummingbirds (Trochilidae)

Hummingbirds are found only in the western hemisphere and, of the approximately 338 species, the majority occur in South America, 17 of them in the West Indies. Jamaica has three species, all of which are endemic, at the genus, species or subspecies levels.

Jamaican Mango *(Anthracothorax mango)*

Doctorbird, Mango Hummingbird   13 cm (5 in)   Plate 23

Status Common resident, but not as abundant as the other species.

Identification A large dark hummingbird with a long black, slightly decurved bill. Eye dark brown. Head and back greeny-bronze washed with magenta on upper back and wing coverts. Two central tail feathers black, the rest are iridescent rusty-purple-blue bordered by black scallops (immature females have a terminal border of white which wears to a few spots in adults). Sides of head and neck are iridescent magenta. Underparts of throat to vent black (in immatures the gorget is blue, rest of underparts brown). Undertail coverts are bluish-green. There are two white spots on flanks. Females are a paler version of male.

Voice A raspy, tuneless 'chi-chi-chi-chi-chi', or a sound similar to kissing tongue to palate.

Habitat Abundant in open, arid areas in the lowlands and near the coast. Rarer in upland areas.

Habits Feeds on insects and nectar of flowers of many trees and plants such as banana, coffee, cactus, and *Bauhinia*. Nests year-round, in *Casuarina*, Mangrove, French Peanut, Cashaw trees. Nest placed above eye-level, saddled on branches.

Range Jamaica, an endemic species.

Plate 23 Jamaican Mango

Red-billed (or Western) Streamertail
(Trochilus polytmus polytmus)
DOCTORBIRD, SCISSORS-TAIL, LONG-TAIL HUMMINGBIRD   13–30.5 cm (5–12 in)

Plates 24 & 25

Status Common resident.

Identification *Male* Head black, lateral crown feathers and ear coverts elongated beyond nape. Body bright iridescent emerald green, darker on back. Wings brown, tail black shot with green, *the second to outermost tail feathers very long* (13 cm (6 in) or more) forming the 'streamers' which are scalloped and fluted on the inside and create a high whining hum in flight. The streamers are often crossed. Immature males and males in moult lack the streamers. *Bill is red with a black tip*, older birds have more red. *Female* Head grey in adult, brown in immature. Back is green, underparts are white, lightly spotted with green at sides of breast. No streamers, but the outer tail feathers are broadly tipped white. Upper mandible is reddish black with a small area of red. Lower mandible has some red in centre and at base.

Plate 24 Red-billed Streamertail – female

Voice Loud 'chink, chink, chink' or 'tsee, tsee' or 'teet, teet'.

Habitat Abundant and widespread, from sea level to the highest mountains wherever there are flowers. Absent from eastern Jamaica.

Habits Feeds on nectar and small insects, fruit-flies and swarming ants. Nests year-round but chiefly Jan–Jun. Nest is a tiny cup of plant fibres bound together with cobweb and decorated with lichen.

Range Jamaica. An endemic genus, species and subspecies.

Plate 25 Red-billed Streamertail – male

Black-billed (or Eastern) Streamertail
(Trochilus polytmus scitulus)

<small>DOCTORBIRD</small>   23–26 cm (9–10 in)   Plate 26

Status   Less abundant than the Red-billed Streamertail.

Identification   Male, female and immature are similar to Red-billed Streamertail but slightly smaller, more blue-green in colour and with completely black bills. Bill is also narrower at base.

Voice   Similar to the Red-billed Streamertail.

Habitat   Only found in the humid eastern section of Jamaica, from Port Antonio (particularly the San San area) east to Bowden on the southeast coast and in the John Crow Mountains, Cornpuss Gap and Bath. Rarely found with Red-billed Streamertails except where their ranges overlap.

Habits   Feeding habits are similar to Red-billed Streamertail.

Range   Jamaica, an endemic genus, species and subspecies.

Plate 26   Black-billed Streamertail – male

Vervain Hummingbird *(Mellisuga minima)*

LITTLE DOCTORBIRD, BEE HUMMINGBIRD   5 cm (2 in)   Plates 27 & 28

Status   Very common resident.

Identification   A minute hummingbird. Head and back green, underparts white, sides of breast lightly spotted with green. The female's tail is rounded and broadly tipped white on outer tail feathers.

Voice   Has a distinct song, a prolonged twittering, sung by the male from an exposed perch.

Habitat   Common in gardens, forest edges and roadsides. Attracted to smaller flowers than the other two species, e.g. Vervain, Tamarind, Pentas and Chinese Hat.

Habits   They often hover with tail tilted up. Wings sound like the buzz of bees. Mating display more obvious than the other hummers: two birds rise together face to face to a great height twittering and sometimes clutching each other by the feet and tumbling head over heels to the ground, or parting at the top of flight and falling away in an arc in different directions. Aggressive behaviour is similar to mating behaviour but is usually performed by two of the same sex. Nests year-round, chiefly Dec–May.

Range   Jamaica. *Mellisuga m.minima* is an endemic subspecies. Another race inhabits Hispaniola and adjacent small islands.

Plate 27   Vervain Hummingbird – male

Plate 28   Vervain Hummingbird – female

Todies (Todidae)

Todies belong to an insectivorous family of five species which is restricted to the Greater Antilles. One endemic species is found in Jamaica.

Jamaican Tody *(Todus todus)*

ROBIN REDBREAST   9 cm (3.5 in)   Plate 29

Status   Common resident.

Identification   A small, round, leaf-green bird with a *red throat*, grey eye with broken red eye ring and long, broad bill usually tilted up. The lower mandible is red. Breast white washed with green, rest of underparts pale yellow, with pink flanks. Legs brown. Wings and tail black edged green.

Voice   Alarm is a hissing 'cheep'. Call a throaty rattly 'frrrup'.

Habitat   Found in all types of forest from mangroves to the mountains, but most common at mid-levels.

Habits   Sits under foliage with head inclined upwards searching the underside of leaves for insects. Flies from one perch to another with a buzzy noise of the wings. Excavates nest-holes (Dec–Jul) in steep banks, and in rotten tree-trunks. Eats moths and caterpillars, which it kills by battering, and occasionally berries.

Range   Jamaica. An endemic species.

Kingfishers Alcedinidae

Of six species found in the New World, only one, a winter visitor, is seen in Jamaica. They hover and plunge-dive into fresh or salt water to catch fish.

Belted Kingfisher *(Ceryle alcyon)*

KINGFISHER   30.5 cm (12 in)

Common winter visitor (Aug–Apr) near streams, ponds, dams, reservoirs and sea coasts. Female has two breast bands, one grey and one rufous, male has only the grey band.

Voice   A loud rattle, not unlike the Loggerhead Kingbird, but harsher.

Range   North America, wintering to South America via the West Indies and Central America.

Plate 29   Jamaican Tody

Woodpeckers (Picidae)

Woodpeckers are one of the families that are particularly well-distributed in the West Indies (12 species). One endemic species and one winter visitor occur regularly in Jamaica.

Jamaican Woodpecker *(Melanerpes radiolatus)*

<small>WOODPECKER</small>   Male: 24 cm (9.5 in)   Plate 30
                                                Female: 23 cm (9 in)   Plate 31

Status   Common and widespread resident.
Identification   Forehead, face and throat cream. *Crown red (m), brownish-olive (f)*. Nape bright scarlet. Bill black. Eye crimson. Upper back and wings with narrow black and white bars, which get wider on rump. *Breast brownish-olive, centre of abdomen bright orange* bordered with orange-yellow and buff. Flanks and undertail coverts barred black and white washed with orange-yellow. Tail black. Legs black.
Voice   Loud, rolling 'chee-ee-erp', not unlike the parakeet. Sometimes a fairly rapid 'churp-churp-churp'.
Habitat   Wooded areas, forests, cultivations and gardens, from sea level to the mountains.

Plate 30   Jamaican Woodpecker – female at nest

Habits Flight undulating. Usually the loud drumming or tapping on trees, or loud cry, attract attention. Often seen hopping up and down the trunks and branches of trees probing for insects under the bark or in rotten wood. Nests in holes excavated in dead trees or rotten telegraph poles, and feeds the young on insects and fruit. Two broods are raised (Dec–Aug).

Range Jamaica. An endemic species.

Plate 31 Jamaican Woodpecker – male at nest

Yellow-bellied Sapsucker *(Sphyrapicus varius)*

SAPSUCKER, SPANISH WOODPECKER   20 cm (8 in)

Uncommon winter visitor (Oct–Mar) in forest edges and gardens island-wide. Drills holes in trees to which it returns regularly and annually.

Voice   A loud 'mew'.

Range   North America, wintering in South and Central America, the Bahamas and Greater Antilles.

Tyrant Flycatchers (Tyrannidae)

Nine species nest on the island; four are endemic species, four endemic subspecies and one is a summer resident. In addition the Eastern Wood-Pewee is a vagrant. Some species are called 'Tom Fool' in Jamaica because of their apparent lack of caution.

Jamaican Elaenia *(Myiopagis cotta)*

SARAH BIRD, YELLOW-CROWNED ELAENIA   12.5 cm (5 in)   Plate 32

Status   Uncommon resident.

Identification   Upper parts brownish olive, darker on head with a *concealed orange-yellow crown patch* (absent in immature), *pale yellowish-white or white superciliary stripe, small black bill*, brown eye. Wings brownish-olive edged with greenish-olive, more noticeable in centre of wing, *no wing bars*. Tail long, square, brownish-olive edged olive-yellow. Throat grey, rest of underparts pale yellow in adults; in immatures the underparts are greyish white, becoming yellow in ventral area. Legs dark brown.

Voice   A fast 'ti-si-si-sip' or 'si-si-si-sip', or 'si-sip'.

Habitat   Forest and bushy areas, coffee fields, from lowlands to the mountains, Paradise, Cockpit Country, Anchovy, Mandeville, Hardwar Gap and Mona Woods.

Habits   Inconspicuous and difficult to locate. More often heard than seen. Picks insects off leaves and twigs or catches them in mid-air. Also eats berries. Nest cup-shaped, well-hidden in bunches of seed pods or in Spanish Moss (Mar–Jun).

Range   Jamaica. An endemic species.

Plate 32 Jamaican Elaenia

Greater Antillean Elaenia *(Elaenia fallax)*

SARAH BIRD   15 cm (6 in)   Plate 33

Status   Locally common resident.

Identification   Upper parts dark olive brown. Head grey, lighter around eye with a *dark line through eye*. Concealed *crown patch white* (absent in immature). Bill is small, dark grey, with base of lower mandible pale pinkish. Wings grey, edged white forming 'V's on back. Wing coverts edged greenish-white forming *two distinct wing bars*. Tail long, grey, slightly forked and almost translucent. Neck and breast pale yellow, indistinctly streaked grey, rest of underparts pale yellow.

Voice   'Pwee-chi-chi-chiup', 'see-ere, chewit-chewit'.

Habitat   Forest edges (Apr–Oct) in the Port Royal Mountains, Blue Mountains, and higher hills of St Andrew. (Nov–Mar) scattered thinly throughout the island. In winter months is inconspicuous, silent and rarely seen.

Habits   Feeds like a warbler on insects. Also eats berries. Nests (May–Jun) high in trees, a cup-shaped nest of moss.

Range   Jamaica. *E.f.fallax* is an endemic subspecies. Another subspecies inhabits Hispaniola.

Greater Antillean Pewee *(Contopus caribaeus)*

WILLIE PEE, LITTLE TOM FOOL   15 cm (6 in)   Plate 34

Status   Common resident.

Identification   Upper parts dark olive-brown, darker on head. Eye dark brown. Bill is broad, flat, upper mandible brown, lower mandible clay-coloured. Wings brown, light buff wing bars indistinct or absent. Tail is as long as body, brown and slightly forked. Breast and sides light brown, centre of abdomen buffy-yellow shading to buff undertail coverts. Legs dark brown. *Immatures* Throat to vent grey, paler over breastbone. Lower mandible pale horn colour.

Voice   A plaintive 'pee' at varying tonal levels. Rarely 'pee-wee' is heard. Also 'weep', 'ee-oo', 'chick'.

Habitat   Chiefly mid-level forest edges, e.g. Hardwar Gap, Mandeville, Anchovy, descending to lower elevations in winter months.

Habits   Feeds on insects which it catches with an audible snap of the beak, and returns to the same or another nearby perch. Usually *flickers tail on landing*. Nests (Apr–Jun), possibly twice a year, in the fork of a tree. Nest is cup-shaped, made of grass, straw and *Tillandsia* roots.

Range   Jamaica. *Contopus c. pallidus* is an endemic subspecies. Also the Bahamas, Cuba, Hispaniola and adjacent small islands.

Plate 33   Greater Antillean Elaenia

Plate 34   Greater Antillean Pewee

Sad Flycatcher *(Myiarchus barbirostris)*

LITTLE TOM FOOL, DUSKY-CAPPED FLYCATCHER 16.5 cm (6.5 in) Plates 35 & 36

Status   Common resident.

Identification   The smallest of the three Jamaican Myiarchus Fly-catchers. In *adults* the upper parts are brownish-olive, tail edged finely with rufous. The throat is greyish white, rest of underparts lemon yellow. Wings and greater wing coverts are edged buff (more indistinct than in Stolid Flycatcher). Bill is dark and broad, lower mandible buff at base. Legs black. In *immatures* the breast and throat are greyish-white, and only the ventral area is yellow.

Voice   'Pip', 'pip-pip' sometimes 'pip-pip-pireee' rising at the end.

Habitat   Upper and mid-level hills and mountains. Descends to lower elevations in winter when found in citrus groves, mangrove and sea-level forests.

Habits   Flies out from a perch to feed on small insects and returns to the same area. Nests (Apr–Jun) in holes in trees, rotten fence posts, bamboo joints or birdhouses, sometimes in eaves of houses.

Range   Jamaica. An endemic species.

Plate 35   Sad Flycatcher – side view

Plate 36 Sad Flycatcher – front view

Rufous-Tailed Flycatcher *(Myiarchus validus)*

BIG TOM FOOL   24 cm (9.5 in)   Plates 37 & 38

Status   Fairly common resident.

Identification   Head and back olive brown. Bill is large, wide, flat and black. Wings and tail are brown edged with orange-rufous. *No wing bars.* Underparts grey becoming yellow in ventral area. Legs greyish-brown.

Voice   A fast, rolling 'pree-ee-ee-ee-ee', 'chi-chi-chiup'.

Habitat   Wooded hills and mountains.

Habits   Does not flush easily. Nests in cavities in trees and rotten fence posts. Feeds on insects and berries, e.g. of Red Birch, Sweetwood and Bitterwood.

Range   Jamaica. An endemic species.

Plate 37   Rufous-tailed Flycatcher front view

Plate 38   Rufous-tailed Flycatcher rear view

Stolid Flycatcher *(Myiarchus stolidus)*

Tom Fool   20 cm (8 in)   Plate 39

Status   Common resident.

Identification   Head olive-brown, upper parts olive-grey. Tail brown, inner web clay-coloured (sometimes quite rufous). Wings brown with white edges (more distinctly marked than Sad Flycatcher). Two *white wing bars*. Throat and breast white, rest of underparts pale yellow.

Voice   A prolonged rolling 'whee-ee-ee', 'swee-ip', 'bzzzrt'.

Habitat   Chiefly arid woodland, mangrove forest and scrub, but in very dry weather may be found further inland. Common on Clarendon Plains.

Habits   Does not flush easily. Eats butterflies and other insects as well as berries. Nest is similar to that of Sad Flycatcher.

Range   Jamaica. *M.s.stolidus* is an endemic subspecies. Other races are found in the Bahamas and in the Greater and Lesser Antilles.

Plate 39   Stolid Flycatcher

Jamaican Becard *(Pachyramphus niger)*

JUDY (m), MOUNTAIN DICK (f), RICKATEE   18 cm (7 in)   Plates 40, 41 & 42

Status   Widespread, locally common resident.

Identification   *Male* Glossy black above, duller below, with a concealed white spot in scapulars, usually visible only in flight. Head comparatively large, bill is thick and black; eye large and brown. Tail slightly forked. *Female and immature* Head, upper breast and wings are bright rufous, back and tail grey. Underparts pale pinkish buff shading to grey with a yellowish wash on undertail coverts.

Voice   A melodious 'ricka-ticky-ti-tee' rising on last note.

Habitat   Edges or open parts of wooded hills, or pastures with large trees. Most common at mid-levels, but also found in the mountains.

Habits   Usually first located by call. Feeds on insects and berries. Forages in upper and mid-levels of tall trees (Sweetwood, Prickly Yellow). Nests (Mar–Jun) building an enormous nest of skeletonised leaves, grasses, ferns and vines, and sometimes completely of Usnea moss, hanging at the end of a slender branch. The entrance is at the bottom.

Range   Jamaica. An endemic species.

Plate 40   Jamaican Becard – female

Plate 41   Jamaican Becard – male

Plate 42   Nest of Jamaican Becard

Loggerhead Kingbird *(Tyrannus caudifasciatus)*
LOGGERHEAD   20.5 cm (8 in)   Plate 43

Status   Common and widespread.

Identification   *Adult* Head to below eye black with a concealed orange-yellow crown patch exposed during display. Eye dark brown. Back grey. Tail square, black with white base, and tipped with off-white. Wings black, secondaries and secondary coverts have narrow white edges. In breeding plumage the undertail coverts and base of tail feathers are tinged with pale yellow. *Immature* Crown patch white. Tail tipped with buff. Wings black, secondaries and secondary coverts narrowly edged with cream.

Voice   Song 'P-P-Q' or 'P-P-U' in breeding season (Nov–Jul). Usually a loud rolling chatter.

Habitat   Forest edges, orange groves, gardens and road edges. Often seen perched on electric wires.

Habits   Nest (Nov–Jul) cup-shaped, made of seed pods, stems, grass, string etc.

Range   Jamaica. *T.c.jamaicensis* is an endemic subspecies. Other sub-species inhabit the Bahamas and other Greater Antillean islands.

Plate 43   Loggerhead Kingbird

Gray Kingbird *(Tyrannus dominicensis)*
PETCHARY   23 cm (9 in)

Common summer resident in open wooded areas, cultivations and gardens. Told from the Loggerhead Kingbird by *dark mask extending from ear coverts through eye to beak* and by *slightly forked tail*. Arrives in March to nest, usually at the base of coconut or palm fronds, leaving in early October, when it is common in mangrove forests near the coast. Rarely a few spend the winter. Very noisy and aggressive, often seen chasing Turkey Vultures, hawks and other birds.

Voice   Loud emphatic 'pitch-errie', and a wide variety of other notes.

Range   North America, Bahamas, West Indies and mainland coasts around the Caribbean. A permanent resident from Hispaniola east and south to northern South America.

Swallows (Hirundinidae)

Swallows have long pointed wings, and small beaks with wide gapes for catching flying insects. They are often seen in mixed flocks with swifts. Three species nest in Jamaica and others occur as transients in the winter.

Northern Rough-winged Swallow *(Stelgidopteryx serripennis)*
.   12.5 cm (5 in)

Rare transient (Aug–Nov, Jan–Apr) in small numbers, usually seen with Cave Swallows over wet fields or marshes or on electric wires near the coast.

Range   North and Central America, wintering in Central America and casually in the Greater Antilles.

Bank Swallow *(Riparia riparia)*
12.5 cm (5 in)

Rare transient (Sep and Jan) seen at Tryall and Elim.

Range   North America and Europe. North American migrants winter in South America via the West Indies.

Cave Swallow *(Hirundo fulva)*
SWALLOW, RAIN BIRD   12.5 cm (5 in)

Common resident. Nests Oct–May under cliffs, in caves and under bridges
and buildings. *Tail unforked.*
Voice 'Tit-swee' or 'wit-wit'.
Range   Greater Antilles except the Cayman Islands. Also North, Central
and South America.

Barn Swallow *(Hirundo rustica)*
15 cm (6 in)

Common transient (Aug–Nov and Jan–Apr) over airports, golf courses,
wet meadows, all around the island. *Deeply forked tail*, blue back and
cinnamon underparts distinguish it from the Caribbean Martin.
Range   Worldwide. North American residents winter to South America
via Central America and the West Indies.

Tree Swallow *(Tachycineta bicolor)*
12.5 cm (5 in)

Common winter transient (Jan–Apr), Negril, Treasure Beach, Hardwar
Gap in small numbers.
Range   North America, wintering south to northern South America via
the Bahamas, Greater Antilles and Central America.

Golden Swallow *(Tachycineta euchrysea)*
RAIN BIRD, SWALLOW   12.5 cm (5 in)

Status Very rare resident. Was plentiful up to the end of the last
century.
Identification A *small iridescent green swallow with snowy white under-
parts*. Similar to the migrant Tree Swallow but tail is more deeply forked.
Golden glints on lower back seen when flying away.
Voice A soft twittering Apr–Jun, but usually silent.
Habitat Canefields on the edge of the Cockpit Country, Windsor and
Barbecue Bottom, Nov–Jan and Jul–Aug.
Habits Swoops low over hills and canefields. Said to nest in caves or on
buildings but no recent record.
Range   Jamaica. *T.e.euchrysea* is an endemic subspecies. Another race is
found in Hispaniola.

Caribbean Martin *(Progne dominicensis)*

SWALLOW   20.5 cm (8 in)   Plates 44 & 45

Status Locally common summer resident.

Identification *Male* A large blue-black swallow with a slightly forked tail and white underparts. The blue of the head ends in a sharply defined line on the upper breast, and there is a dark band along the flanks under the wing. Undertail coverts are lightly tipped with blue-black. *Females and immatures* Brown above with some blue in wing coverts.

Voice A liquid 'chileet, chur-chur, chi-chi-chiwee'.

Habitat Often seen near the coast, e.g. Treasure Beach, Parrottee, Wallywash, Negril, Bluefields, Feb–Oct perched on power lines.

Habits Nests Apr–Jun in old woodpecker holes in coconut palms or telegraph poles, or at the top of dead coconut trees. More than one pair uses a hole.

Range *P.d.dominicensis* West Indies. Other subspecies are found in Cuba and the Isle of Pines, and Mexico. Winters (presumably) in South America.

Plate 44 Caribbean Martin – male and **Plate 45** (inset) female

Crows (Corvidae)

Crows are to be found worldwide except in Central and South America. There are four species in the West Indies, one of which is endemic to Jamaica.

Jamaican Crow *(Corvus jamaicensis)*

JABBERING CROW, JAMMING CROW, JAMICROW   38 cm (15 in)   Plate 46

Status Locally common. May be extending its range in Westmoreland and Manchester.
Identification A large, sooty black bird with heavy black bill.
Voice Harsh 'caw caw' calls and loud jabbering and gobbling.
Habitat Wet mid-level limestone forest. Most easily seen in the Cockpit Country, and near Good Hope; also Moneague, Worthy Park and in the John Crow Mountains. Not found in the Blue Mountains.
Habits Usually located by calls. Omnivorous: fruits, eggs, lizards. Forages in bromeliads and under bark for amphibians, crabs, larvae, grubs and water. Nest (Apr–Jun) a roughly built platform high in a tall tree.
Range Jamaica. An endemic species.

Plate 46 Jamaican Crow

Thrushes (Turdidae)

Three thrushes breed on the island, two are endemic and one is an endemic subspecies. Three species are rare transients.

Veery *(Catharus fuscescens)*

15 cm (6 in)

Rare transient (Jan–Apr) Mona, Hardwar Gap, Malvern.
Range North America. Winters in South America, usually via Central America, but rarely through the Bahamas and Greater Antilles.

Gray-cheeked Thrush *(Catharus minimus)*

15 cm (6 in)

Rare transient (Oct–Dec) Mona, Hardwar Gap, Malvern.
Range North America and north-eastern Siberia. North American residents winter in northern South America via the Bahamas and Greater Antilles.

Swainson's Thrush *(Catharus ustulatus)*

15 cm (6 in)

Rare transient (Sep, Oct, Apr) Anchovy, Hardwar Gap, Malvern.
Range North America, wintering in Central and South America chiefly via Central America, rarely via the Bahamas and Greater Antilles.

Rufous-throated Solitaire *(Myadestes genibarbis)*

SOLITAIRE, MOUNTAIN WHISTLER, FIDDLER   19 cm (7.5 in)   Plate 47

Status Fairly common resident.
Identification *Adult Head and back dark grey, a white crescent below eye* and a white spot on the chin and on either side of bill. Eyes brown. *Throat and undertail coverts chestnut*, abdomen grey. Tail grey with *three outer tail feathers mostly white*. Wings grey edged with white. *Legs yellow. Immature* Head and back dark grey *spotted with rufous*. Wing coverts tipped with cinnamon. Crescent below eye is salmon-coloured.
Voice Song in summer variable, slow flutelike whistles and trills. Winter call a single long 'toot' like a distant car horn, as well as other short calls.

Plate 47   Rufous-throated Solitaire

Habitat   In summer (Apr–Nov) found in mountain forests. In winter most descend to lower elevations.

Habits   Difficult to locate because it is a ventroloquist, but will often be found feeding in or under a fruiting tree. Eats fruit, berries and insects. Nest (Apr–Aug) is cup-shaped, placed in a cavity, in a tree-fern, creeper or bromeliad.

Range   Jamaica. *M.g.solitarius* is an endemic subspecies. Other races inhabit Hispaniola, Dominica, Martinique, St Lucia and rarely St Vincent.

White-eyed Thrush *(Turdus jamaicensis)*

GLASS-EYE, SHINE-EYE   23 cm (9 in)   Plate 48

Status   Fairly common resident.

Identification   *Adult   Entire head bright rufous-brown. Eye is greyish-white*, bill black. Throat is white streaked with rufous-brown, upper breast white, lower breast and sides grey, fading to whitish on mid-abdomen. Undertail coverts white with grey centres. Legs and tail medium brown. *Immatures*   Lack streaking on throat, but are *heavily streaked on breast*.

Voice   Song is varied and musical, each phrase repeated two or three times, with an oft-repeated 'hee-haw' whistle. Call and alarm notes are harsh and shrill.

Habitat   Forested gullies, hills and mountains, e.g. Hardwar Gap, Blue Mountains, Mandeville. Descends to lower elevations in cooler months.

Habits   Feeds on fruit and insects from tops of trees to ground level. Difficult to see in thick canopy but sometimes descends to lower shrubbery or roads. Nest (Apr–Jun) is cup-shaped.

Range   Jamaica. An endemic species.

Plate 48   White-eyed Thrush

White-chinned Thrush *(Turdus aurantius)*

Status   Very common resident.

Identification   *Adult* Dark grey upper parts with a *conspicuous white spot in wing*. The 'white chin' is small. Underparts lighter grey with centre of abdomen white, undertail coverts grey with white tips, tail plain black. *Legs and bill are burnt orange*, bill tipped black. Eye chestnut. *Immatures* are darker browny-grey on breast, with streaked abdomen and grey lower underparts, a few white flecks in undertail coverts.

Voice   Varied, from a melodious lullaby in the breeding season to shrill whistles 'p'lice, p'lice' and chicken-like clucking repeated for long periods.

Habitat   Wooded hills and mountains, but occurs at sea level on the north and southwestern coasts.

Habits   Most often seen hopping across country roads, *tail held high*. Feeds on lizards, insects and berries. Nests May-Jul at the base of coconut fronds and in shrubs.

Range   Jamaica. An endemic species.

Plate 49   White-chinned Thrush

Mimic Thrushes (Mimidae)

Three species of this small New World family occur in Jamaica, including one migrant and two residents. They make up in song for their lack of colourful plumage, some even singing at night, hence their local name of 'Nightingale'.

Bahama Mockingbird *(Mimus gundlachii)*
HILL'S MOCKINGBIRD, SALT ISLAND NIGHTINGALE, SPANISH NIGHTINGALE

28 cm (11 in)   Plate 50

Status   Locally common resident.
Identification   Noticeably larger and browner than the Northern Mockingbird, with mottling on face and a blackish whisker on throat. Underparts whitish, streaked brownish at sides of breast and abdomen. Undertail coverts mottled. Wing coverts edged white but *no white flash in wing. Tail tipped with white* except for two central feathers. **NB** *Immature Northern Mockingbirds are streaked on breast.*

Plate 50   Bahama Mockingbird

Voice Similar but richer than the Northern Mockingbird. Does not mimic other birds. Call 'torkey-torkey-torkey-tork, chup chup chup'.

Habitat Restricted to south coastal, dry limestone forest in Hellshire Hills, Portland Ridge and Salt Island Lagoon.

Habits Singing and nesting occur in Feb–Jun. Behaviour is similar to Northern Mockingbird but does not open wings jerkily.

Range South central Jamaica. *M.g.hillii* is an endemic subspecies. Also found in the Bahamas and cays off the northern coast of Cuba.

Northern Mockingbird *(Mimus polyglottos)*

NIGHTINGALE   20.5 cm (8 in)

Very common resident. It is found in winter up to about 600 m (2000 ft) but goes to higher elevations in summer. Raises wings jerkily displaying white wing patch.

Nests Dec–Jun in a thorny cup.

Voice A beautiful songster and expert mimic of other birds. Call note 'peter, peter'. Once young are hatched parents only give location calls and sharp 'chips'. Call of young a penetrating 'pseeent'.

Range *M.p.orpheus* Bahamas and Greater Antilles. Also North America.

Gray Catbird *(Dumetella carolinensis)*

20.5 cm (8 in)

Uncommon winter visitor (Sep–Apr) in thick undergrowth, from whence the 'me-eeew' call first identifies it. Does not sing in winter quarters until just before departure in April.

Range North America and Bermuda. Winters to South America via the Greater Antilles and Central America.

Waxwings (Bombycillidae)

Waxwings are so called because of the red waxy tips to some of the secondaries of adults.

Cedar Waxwing *(Bombycilla cedrorum)*

15 cm (6 in)

Rare spring transient (Dec–Apr) usually seen in flocks from 10–150, e.g. at Mona, Stony Hill, Irish Town, Malvern, Ocho Rios, but not seen every year. Feeds on *Ficus*, Privet and other berries.

Range North America. Winters to northern South America via Bahamas, Central America and western Greater Antilles.

Starlings (Sturnidae)

This is one Old World species that has been introduced and prospered in many countries of the world including Jamaica.

European Starling *(Sturnus vulgaris)*

STARLING   15 cm (6 in)

Introduced into the island in about 1903 and after a slow start has increased in numbers rapidly in the last 25 years. Found chiefly in the lowlands, in parks, gardens and pastures, also at mid-levels. Moves around the island, and is sometimes abundant and sometimes absent from a particular place.

Voice 'Cheer-ear', sometimes uttered as clear human-sounding whistle, rising then falling. Also clicks and grating sounds.

Nests Apr–Jun in natural and artificial cavities and woodpecker holes, sometimes evicting the owners.

Vireos (Vireonidae)

Vireos belong to a small New World family. They are active insect- and berry-eating birds, which are similar to warblers. Often drab and difficult to locate in the thick foliage where they forage, their short-phrased, repetitive songs make their presence obvious. Two endemic species are found in Jamaica, one summer migrant nests on the island and several North American species are winter transients.

White-eyed Vireo *(Vireo griseus)*

15 cm (6 in)

Rare transient (Jan–Mar) in coastal shrubbery.

Range North America, Bermuda and Mexico, wintering south to the Bahamas, Central America and the Greater Antilles.

Philadelphia Vireo *(Vireo philadelphicus)*

12.5 cm (5 in)

Casual transient (Nov–Feb). Seen at Anchovy, Yallahs, Hardwar Gap, Mona.
Range   North America. Winters in Central America, casually via the Bahamas, Cuba and Jamaica.

Red-eyed Vireo *(Vireo olivaceus)*

12.5 cm (5 in)

Regular transient (Sep–Nov), e.g. Anchovy, Hardwar Gap, Mona, Malvern.
Range   North America. Winters in South America via Central America, the Bahamas, Cuba and Jamaica.

Black-whiskered Vireo *(Vireo altiloquus)*
JOHN-TO-WHIT, JOHN CHEWIT   12.5 cm (5 in)

Very common summer resident arriving in March.
Nest   A pendant cup suspended from a forked branch. Found through-out the island in open woodland and gardens at all elevations.
Voice   'John Chewit', 'Sweet John', 'Chewit John' and sometimes the full 'Sweet John Chewit' is repeated endlessly. The typical song is replaced by a location 'skwee' note after the young are hatched in July and until the birds leave in early Oct.
Range   *V.a.altiloquus*   Greater Antilles except Cuba and the Isle of Pines, Cayman, the Swan Islands and St Croix. Winters in northern South America. Some permanent residents in Hispaniola. Other subspecies inhabit other West Indian islands.

Jamaican Vireo *(Vireo modestus)*
SEWI-SEWI, WHITE-EYED VIREO   11.5 cm (4.5 in)   Plate 51

Status   Very common.
Identification   *Adult Head is plain greenish-olive. Bill is pinkish-brown,* paler below. Iris is very pale grey *(appearing white)*. Back is olive, wings dark grey tinged with green. *Two greenish-white wing bars.* Tail is square with greenish edges. Legs are blue-grey. Underparts are entirely yellow. *Immature* Head is grey. Iris is greyish-brown. Only the centre of under-parts is yellow, rest is greyish. Immature is sometimes confused with immature Arrow-headed Warbler but the latter has a dark line through eye and flirts its tail down.

Voice A wide variety of songs, e.g. 'sewi-sewi', 'wichy-wichy-woo', which it changes frequently but repeats for minutes at a time. The song is often echoed by a mate foraging nearby. Has a loud scold note, a fast 'chi-chi-chi-chi-chi'.

Habitat Bushy areas, forest edges and roadsides, at all elevations.

Habits Difficult to see as it flits rapidly about in overgrown bush constantly flirting tail up. Feeds on insects and berries. Nest (Apr–Jun) is pendant, suspended from a forked branch, constructed of fern or *Tillandsia* stalks and decorated with lichen.

Range Jamaica. An endemic species.

Plate 51 Jamaican Vireo

Blue Mountain Vireo *(Vireo osburni)*

12.5 cm (5 in)   Plate 52

Status   Uncommon.

Identification   A rather chunky grey bird with a proportionately *heavy black bill. No wing bars.* Underparts: *adults* pale yellow; *immatures* light grey becoming pale yellow towards tail. Eye reddish brown.

Voice   A rolling whistle. Alarm call a harsh trill.

Habitat   Mountain forests in moist areas such as John Crow and Blue Mountain ranges, Cockpit Country, Mount Diablo.

Habits   Feeds among leaves and is more often heard than seen. Nest like Jamaican Vireo but larger.

Range   Jamaica. An endemic species.

Plate 52   Blue Mountain Vireo

Emberizidae

This large family includes six subfamilies: wood warblers (Parulinae), bananaquits (Coerebinae), tanagers (Thraupinae), grosbeaks and buntings (Cardinalinae), grassquits, finches and sparrows (Emberizinae), and blackbirds and orioles (Icterinae). These will be treated separately.

WOOD WARBLERS (PARULINAE)

Wood warblers are only found in the Americas and are not related to Old World warblers. Two species are resident in Jamaica, the Yellow Warbler and the endemic Arrow-headed Warbler. The others, called 'Christmas Birds', 'Chip chip birds' or 'Check, check birds' are small colourful migrants from North America. Some spend the winter in Jamaica and some go farther south. Some warblers are difficult to identify when they arrive in August or September because they are in immature plumage. In the winter they do not usually sing except just after arrival or just before departure, but make distinctive chipping notes by which some species can be identified.

Tennesee Warbler *(Vermivora peregrina)*
11 cm (4.25 in)

Rare winter visitor (Oct–Mar) in lowland gardens and mountain forest.
Range   North America wintering through Central America and the West Indies to northern South America.

Northern Parula *(Parula americana)*
9.5 cm (3.75 in)

Fairly common winter visitor (Aug–May) in gardens and woodlands.
Range   North America, wintering in Central America and the West Indies.

Yellow Warbler *(Dendroica petechia)*
MANGROVE WARBLER, MANGROVE CANARY, GOLDEN WARBLER   10 cm (4 in)

Common resident.
Nests   Apr–Jun in mangroves and scrub forest near coast and along rivers.
Range   *D.p.eoa* Jamaica and the Cayman Islands. Also breeds in North and Central America, the Bahamas, and throughout the Caribbean.

Chestnut-sided Warbler *(Dendroica pensylvanica)*

11 cm (4.25 in)

Rare autumn transient (Sep–Oct) in non-breeding plumage.
Range   North America wintering in Central America.

Magnolia Warbler *(Dendroica magnolia)*

11 cm (4.25 in)

Uncommon winter visitor (Nov–May) in gardens and orchards.
Range   North America, wintering in the Bahamas, Greater Antilles, Central and South America.

Cape May Warbler *(Dendroica tigrina)*

11 cm (4.25 in)

Common winter visitor (Aug–May) in open wooded areas at all elevations. Feeds at hummingbird feeders and comes into houses in search of spiders and their prey.
Range   North America, wintering in the Bahamas and Greater Antilles and rarely in Central America.

Black-throated Blue Warbler *(Dendroica caerulescens)*

11.5 cm (4.5 in)

Common winter visitor (Sep–May) in gardens and woodlands at all elevations. *Female* could be mistaken for an immature Bananaquit.
Range   North America, wintering in the Bahamas, West Indies and Central America.

Yellow-rumped Warbler *(Dendroica coronata)*
MYRTLE WARBLER   12 cm (4.75 in)

Common winter visitor (Oct–May) in some years and scarce in others. Found in *Cashaw* trees, scrub in dry limestone forest, and sometimes in gardens.
Range   North America, wintering in the Bahamas, West Indies, and Central America south to Columbia.

Arrow-headed Warbler *(Dendroica pharetra)*

ANTS BIRD, ANTS PICKER 12.5 cm (5 in) Plates 53, 54 & 55

Status Locally common.

Identification *Adult male* Head and upper back heavily streaked black and white, more finely on head. Rest of upper parts olive-brown with a little white in tail. *Throat to abdomen is spotted with dark grey arrow-heads* which point to the bill and are smaller on the face and throat. Lower underparts are white streaked with buff on undertail coverts. Eye is dark brown and eye ring is white. A dark line runs through the eye. Bill is dark grey, paler below. Wings are brownish olive with two narrow white wing bars. Legs are light grey. *Adult female* is grey and white. *Similar species* to adults is the *Black-and-white Warbler* which is a winter visitor and has three broad white stripes on head. *Immature* has olive back with yellow flecks; two indistinct cream wing bars, yellowish eye ring, black line through eye. Underparts are yellow with grey smudges. There is a little white in tail. *Similar species to immature* is the *Jamaican Vireo* which has plain grey head, pinkish bill; no white in tail. *Constantly flirts tail up.* Eye colour unreliable (see immature Jamaican Vireo).

Plate 53 Arrow-headed Warbler – male

Plate 54   Arrow-headed Warbler – female

Plate 55   Arrow-headed Warbler – immature

Voice   A high metallic 'tick, tick, tick' and a high-pitched squeaky song.
Habitat   Humid forest at all elevations, Hardwar Gap, Cockpit Country. Mandeville, Anchovy, in dense vegetation.
Habits   Feeds on insects. Forages under leaves, on branches and in vines. Unlike the migrant Black-and-white Warbler it is seldom seen on the trunks of trees. Flirts tail down. Nests May–June in a cup-shaped nest of grasses and ferns well concealed in moss.
Range   Jamaica, an endemic species.

Black-throated Green Warbler *(Dendroica virens)*
11 cm (4.25 in)

Uncommon winter visitor (Sep–May) chiefly in upland forests.
Range North America, wintering mostly in Central America, also in the Bahamas and the Greater Antilles.

Blackburnian Warbler *(Dendroica fusca)*
11 cm (4.25 in)

Rare winter transient (Oct–Nov and Apr–May).
Range North America, wintering through Central America, Bahamas, Greater Antilles to South America.

Yellow-throated Warbler *(Dendroica dominica)*
11.5 cm (4.5 in)

Uncommon winter visitor (Sep–May) in forests at all elevations.
Range North America, wintering to the Bahamas, Greater Antilles and Central America.

Prairie Warbler *(Dendroica discolor)*
10 cm (4 in)

Common winter visitor (Jul–May) in woods, gardens and orchards at all elevations.
Range North America, wintering to the Bahamas, the West Indies and Central America.

Palm Warbler *(Dendroica palmarum)*
11.5 cm (4.5 in)

Common winter visitor (Sep–May) in grassland, in gardens chiefly in the lowlands and foothills. Usually seen on or near the ground.
Range North America, wintering to the Bahamas and the Greater Antilles.

Bay-breasted Warbler *(Dendroica castanea)*
12 cm (4.75 in)

Regular winter transient (Oct–Nov), usually in non-breeding plumage.
Range North America, wintering in South America via Cuba, Jamaica, Central America and islands in the western Caribbean.

Black-and-white Warbler *(Mniotilta varia)*
ANTS BIRD, ANTS PICKER   11.5 cm (4.5 in)

Common winter visitor (Jul–May) in all types of forests, woods, scrub and secondary growth. Usually found creeping up and down trunks and branches of trees. Told from similar Arrow-headed Warbler by *three white stripes on head, and behaviour.*
Range   North America, wintering to the West Indies, Bahamas, Central America to northern South America.

American Redstart *(Setophaga ruticilla)*
BUTTERFLY BIRD   11.5 cm (4.5 in)

Common winter visitor (Aug–May) in all types of woodland and gardens.
Range   North America, wintering to the Bahamas, West Indies, Central America to northern South America.

Prothonotary Warbler *(Protonotaria citrea)*
                                                             12.5 cm (5 in)

Regular transient (Oct and Mar) usually in coastal areas.
Range   North America, wintering in Central America and northern South America via the West Indies.

Worm-eating Warbler *(Helmitheros vermivorus)*
                                                             11.5 cm (4.5 in)

Uncommon transient and winter visitor (Sep–May) in forests at all elevations.
Range   North America wintering in Central America, the Bahamas and Greater Antilles.

Swainson's Warbler *(Limnothlypis swainsonii)*
                                                             12.5 cm (5 in)

Uncommon winter visitor (Sep–Apr) in mangroves, lowland woods and mountain forest.
Range   North America, wintering in the Bahamas, Greater Antilles and Central America.

Ovenbird *(Seiurus aurocapillus)*

BETSY KICK-UP   12.5 cm (5 in)

Common transient and winter visitor (Sep–May) in all types of forest and gardens. Usually seen on ground walking and jerking tail upwards.
Range North America, wintering in North, Central and northern South America, and the West Indies.

Northern Waterthrush *(Seiurus noveboracensis)*

12.5 cm (5 in)

Common transient and winter visitor (Aug–Apr), south coast wetlands and damp areas islandwide. Easily confused with Louisiana Waterthrush.
Range North America, wintering via Central America, the Bahamas and West Indies to northern South America.

Louisiana Waterthrush *(Seiurus motacilla)*

12.5 cm (5 in)

Regular winter visitor (Aug–Apr), singly or in small numbers on banks of streams in wooded areas. Easily confused with the Northern Waterthrush.
Range North America, wintering in Bermuda, Bahamas, Central America, the West Indies and northern South America.

Common Yellowthroat *(Geothlypis trichas)*

10 cm (4 in)

Common winter visitor (Sep–May) in bushes and hedges from lowland swamps to the mountains.
Range North America, wintering in Central America, the Bahamas and Greater Antilles.

BANANAQUITS (COEREBINAE)

Bananaquits are found throughout the West Indies, but not in Cuba or Swan Island. They vary considerably in colour and song among the islands.

Bananaquit *(Coereba flaveola)*

TEASY, SUGAR BIRD, BEENY BIRD   10 cm (4 in)   Plates 56 & 57

Status   Abundant and widespread resident.

Identification   Upper parts are black with yellow rump and wide white superciliary stripes. Outer tail feathers are tipped white, *bill is shiny black and decurved* with a red spot at base. Throat is dark grey, breast yellow, rest of underparts white. Wings are dark grey, base of primaries white forming a *white wing patch*. Bend of wings yellow. Eye dark brown. Legs medium grey. Sexes alike but superciliary strip of female more grey. *Immature* has yellow superciliary stripe and throat, and is sometimes mistaken for the female Black-throated Blue Warbler because of the white spot in the wing.

Voice   A rapid 'zizizizizizizizizizi' on one tonal level.

Habitat   Ubiquitous. Found wherever flowering plants occur.

Habits   Feeds on nectar (often puncturing the base of flowers), insects and small berries. Comes to hummingbird feeders or basins of sugar. Nests several times a year. Nest is dome-shaped, made of long grasses and the entrance is at the side. Males build separate sleeping nests.

Range   Jamaica. *C.f.flaveola* is an endemic subspecies. Also Central and South America and the West Indies with the exception of Cuba.

Plate 56   Bananaquit – immature

Plate 57 Bananaquit – adult

TANAGERS (THRAUPINAE)

Tanagers are frugivorous birds found only in the Americas, the majority of species living in South and Central America. Two are resident in Jamaica and are endemic at the species or subspecies level, and two are regular transient migrants.

Jamaican Euphonia *(Euphonia jamaica)*
BLUE QUIT, CHO-CHO QUIT, SHORT-MOUTH BLUEQUIT

11.5 cm (4.5 in)   Plates 58 & 59

Status Common resident.

Identification *Male* A *small, chunky blue-grey bird* with a *short stubby grey bill* darker at the tip. Eye reddish brown. Underparts grey, mid-abdomen bright yellow. Undertail coverts beige, flanks greenish-yellow. Wing lining pale yellow. Wings and tail black edged blue. Legs grey. *Female and immature* Head blue-grey, rest of *upper parts olive-green.* Underparts pale grey shading to cream with buff undertail coverts, flanks green. Wings and tail dark grey, edged green.

Plate 58 Jamaican Euphonia – male

Plate 59   Jamaican Euphonia – female

Voice   A rapidly repeated 'chur-chur-chur-chur-chur' like a motor being started, sometimes ending in a rising 'chip'. Song an attractive squeaky warble.

Habitat   Widespread in gardens and open areas with large trees from sea level to the mountains.

Habits   Feeds on berries, especially Jamaican Mistletoe; soft fruit, e.g. Soursop, Guava, Peach; tender young shoots of Cho-cho, buds and flowers. Builds a globular nest of *Tillandsia*, with a side entrance, in a bunch of *Tillandsia*, moss or bromeliads (Mar–May).

Range   Jamaica. An endemic species.

Stripe-headed Tanager *(Spindalis zena)*
Mark Head, Goldfinch, Champa Beeza (St James)

18 cm (7 in)   Plates 60 & 61

Status   Common resident.

Identification   *Male   Head black with broad white superciliary and malar stripes* and a white chin bordered by black throat. Bill thick, dark grey, lower mandible pale. Back olive-yellow becoming orange on rump. Flight feathers and coverts black margined with white or yellow. Tail black, outer feathers tipped white. Breast orange, fading to a mixture of orange and yellow on abdomen, then white to undertail coverts. Legs grey. *Female and immature* Head olive-grey, head stripes mottled indistinctly grey and white. Breast and abdomen olive-yellow with a small orange patch at centre of breast. Back olive-grey becoming yellowish on rump. Tail and wings dark grey with white margins to wings, and outer tail feathers tipped white.

Voice   Very soft 'seep' often given in flight, and other high, fast 'chi-chi-chi-chi-chi' notes.

Habitat   Forest and roadside bushes in hills and mountains, but found locally to sea level on the wetter north and southwest coasts.

Habits   Usually found in pairs or family groups. Feed on berries, flowers and leaves. Nest (Apr–Jul) in a loosely built cup.

Plate 60   Stripe-headed Tanager – male

Range Jamaica. An endemic subspecies *S.z.nigricephala*. It is the largest of the race and, because of distinct differences in females, Bond suggests that three species should be recognised, the Jamaican species being called *Spindalis nigricephala* making it an endemic species. Other subspecies are found in Hispaniola and Puerto Rico; also Bahamas, Grand Cayman, Cuba and Cozumel Island.

Plate 61 Stripe-headed Tanager – female

Summer Tanager *(Piranga rubra)*

16.5 cm (6.5 in)

Rare transient (Oct–Apr). Individuals have been seen for short periods in most of these months at Anchovy, Mona, Kingston and Montego Bay gardens, Hardwar Gap.
Range North America, wintering in Central America south to Bolivia. A rare transient in the Greater Antilles.

Scarlet Tanager *(Piranga olivacea)*

16 cm (6.25 in)

Rare transient (Oct–May). Individuals have been seen for short periods in these months but not every year, at Anchovy, Mona, Kingston, Montego Bay, Mandeville.
Range North America, wintering in Central America south to Panama.

GROSBEAKS AND BUNTINGS (CARDINALINAE)

All members of this subfamily seen in Jamaica are migrants. Only two are seen regularly.

Rose-breasted Grosbeak *(Pheucticus ludovicianus)*

18.5 cm (7.25 in)

Regular winter visitor and transient in small numbers (Oct and Mar). A few spend the winter chiefly in the mountains, e.g. Hardwar Gap, Mandeville, Stony Hill, Montego Bay foothills.
Range North America, wintering south to Peru via the Bahamas, Mexico, Greater Antilles and islands in the western Caribbean.

Indigo Bunting *(Passerina cyanea)*

11.5 cm (4.5 in)

Regular winter visitor in small flocks (Jan–May), Montego Bay, Mona, Anchovy, Stony Hill. Usually found feeding with grassquits.
Range   North America, the Bahamas and Greater Antilles.

GRASSQUITS, FINCHES AND SPARROWS (EMBERIZINAE)

The members of this subfamily are very diverse, some eating seeds, some fruit and some nectar. Some associate in flocks and others do not. Of the eight species that occur in Jamaica, two are endemic genera, the Orangequit *(Euneornis campestris)* being unique in the West Indies. It is tentatively placed in this family, having been classed as a warbler, honey creeper and tanager.

Black-faced Grassquit *(Tiaris bicolor)*
BLACK SPARROW, GRASS BIRD/QUIT, SQUIT   10 cm (4 in)

Common resident, in gardens and open situations. More common around human habitations than the Yellow-faced Grassquit. *Male* Differs from Yellow-faced Grassquit by *lack of yellow markings on black head and breast,* darker olive-brown back, *pinkish grey legs* and buffy undertail coverts. *Female* and *immatures* are similar to Yellow-faced immatures but have pinkish legs and buffy undertail coverts.

Voice 'Whichi? whichi-chi-chi'.

Nests Year-round but chiefly Jan–Jun. A domed nest of grass in vines, trees or bushes.

Range *T.b.marchii* Jamaica, Hispaniola and adjacent islands. Other subspecies occur in the Bahamas, and throughout the Caribbean except on mainland Cuba.

Yellow-faced Grassquit *(Tiaris olivacea)*

GRASS-BIRD, SQUIT   10 cm (4 in)   Plates 62 & 63

Status Locally common resident.

Identification A small olive-brown finch. *Male Forepart of head, face and breast black with yellow superciliary stripe, crescent below eye, and throat patch. Legs grey. Female Superciliary stripe and lower eyelid cream, pale yellow throat patch. Immatures* No markings except a few yellow feathers in bend of wing.

Voice A series of high-pitched trills and 'ticks'.

Habitat Gardens, grasslands (especially with Guinea grass), edges of forests and woods and cleared areas chiefly in the lowlands.

Habits Builds a domed nest with a side entrance, throughout the year but chiefly Jan–May. Often feeds by hopping on to a grass seed-head and weighing it down to the ground where it can be stripped of seeds. Migrates in flocks around the island depending on food availability.

Range *T.o.olivacea* Cuba and cays, Hispaniola and islands, Jamaica, Cayman Islands. Other subspecies inhabit Puerto Rico, Cozumel Island and Central America to northern South America.

Plate 62 Yellow-faced Grassquit – female

Plate 63 Yellow-faced Grassquit – male

Plate 64 Yellow-shouldered Grassquit – male

Yellow-shouldered Grassquit
(Loxipasser anoxanthus)
YELLOW-BACKED FINCH, YELLOW-SHOULDERED FINCH, YELLOW-BACK

10 cm (4 in)   Plates 64 & 65

Status   Locally common resident.

Identification   *Male   Head and breast black* becoming dark grey on abdomen and flanks, with rusty undertail coverts. *Upper back and wing coverts bright yellow* becoming greenish-yellow on rump. Wings and tail dark grey, margined yellow. Legs are brownish-pink. *Female*   Head olive, finely spotted dark grey. Back and wing coverts paler yellow than male, *bend of wing bright yellow*. Underparts grey, lightly washed olive with paler rusty undertail coverts than male. *Immature*   Like female but only the bend of wing is yellow.

Voice   A descending 'chi-chi-chi-chi-chi'.

Habitat   Common in hills and mountains, e.g. Hardwar Gap, Mandeville, Anchovy, Stony Hill, some found at lower elevations in winter.

Habits   Eats berries and seeds, particularly Spanish Needle. Usually found in roadside and garden shrubbery. Nest spherical, in *Citrus,* Cypress trees, bushes and under bromeliads (Mar–Jul). Usually seen in family groups, does not flock.

Range   Jamaica. An endemic genus and species.

Plate 65   Yellow-shouldered Grassquit – female

Grasshopper Sparrow *(Ammodramus savannarum)*
SAVANNA BIRD, GRASS DODGER, GRASS PINK, 'TICHICRO'   12.5 cm (5 in)

Status   Locally common resident.
Identification   Head dark brown with a median white stripe. Face brownish with an ill-defined superciliary stripe. Bill greyish, paler below. Breast buffy. Lower underparts washed grey over buff. Back brownish-grey-buff. Dark spots on wings. Legs pink. Tail short, wings are as long as tail.
Voice   A very high pitched insect-like 'zeeeee-tick-zeeeeeee'.
Habitat   Grassy fields and savannas, particularly with Pangola, African Star and Guinea grasses.
Habits   Feeds on grass seed and insects. Makes a dome-shaped nest under the creeping stems of grass (Apr–Jun).
Range   Jamaica. *A.s.savannarum* is an endemic subspecies. Other races inhabit Hispaniola and Puerto Rico. Also North, Central and northern South America.

Lincoln's Sparrow *(Melospiza lincolnii)*
12 cm (4.75 in)

Probably regular but uncommon winter visitor (Dec–Apr) in high altitude bushy areas, e.g. Hardwar Gap, Blue Mountains.
Range   North America. Winters in southern USA, Central America, the Bahamas and the Greater Antilles.

Greater Antillean Bullfinch *(Loxigilla violacea)*

BLACK SPARROW, JACK SPARROW, COTTON TREE SPARROW

15 cm (6 in)   Plate 66

Status   Common resident.

Identification   *Adult   Glossy black above* and dull black below with *orange-rufous superciliary stripe, throat and undertail coverts.* Leg dusky brown, eye reddish brown. *Bill thick and black. Females*   Duller black than males. *Immatures   Olive-brown above and lighter below* with similar rusty areas on head and undertail coverts. Some breed in this plumage.

Voice   A wheezy, insect-like call but also capable of loud squawks.

Habitat   Bushy areas and forest undergrowth at all elevations, but chiefly in the mountains. Common at Hardwar Gap and in the Cockpit Country.

Habits   Eats the seeds of a variety of wild and cultivated plants as well as buds and petals of flowers; also fruit, e.g. green Plantain, Coffee, Peppers. Nests in a hole in a dead limb (Mar–Jun), lining it with *Tillandsia*, paper-thin bark or other available material.

Range   Jamaica. *L.v.ruficollis* is an endemic subspecies. Other subspecies are found in the Bahamas, Hispaniola and adjacent small islands.

Plate 66   Greater Antillean Bullfinch

Orangequit *(Euneornis campestris)*

ORANGEQUIT, BLUE BAIZE, LONG-MONTH BLUEQUIT, BLUEBIRD,
BLUE BADAS, SWEE   14 cm (5.5 in)   Plates 67 & 68

Status Locally common resident.

Identification *Male* A small streamlined *blue-black bird,* sometimes appearing bright blue in sunlight, with slightly decurved black bill, black legs, and a black line between russet eyes. There is a *rust-coloured rectangular patch on throat. Female and immature* Head bluish-grey washed olive-brown, wings and tail olive-brown edged fawn. Underparts pale grey with indistinct whitish streaking. Legs olive-brown.

Voice A soft high-pitched 'tseet', 'tsit', 'swee'.

Habitat Open woodland, roadside bushes in wet mid-level and mountain areas, e.g. Newcastle/Hardwar Gap, Mandeville, Anchovy. Found at lower elevations in winter.

Habits Feeds on nectar and fruit from low to mid-level in trees and shrubs. Nest a deep, roughly built cup (Apr–Jun).

Range Jamaica. An endemic genus and species.

Plate 67 Orangequit – male

Plate 68 Orangequit – female

Saffron Finch *(Sicalis flaveola)*

CANARY   13.5 cm (5.25 in)   Plates 69 & 70

Status   Common resident.

Identification   *Male   Head orange*, rest of upper parts buffy-yellow, streaked brownish on back. Wings and tail brown edged yellow. *Face and underparts orange-yellow* becoming yellow towards tail. Bill conical, brown upper, cream lower mandible. Legs buff. *Female*   A paler version of male. *Immatures* are *greeny-grey* streaked brown, with white underparts and *a pale yellow band across the breast*.

Voice   Call note a loud 'chip', and song beginning in March 'chup-chip-chup-zeeee', 'chup-zeeee chup-zeeee chup-zeeee'.

Habitat   Open grassy areas, gardens, from sea level to the mountains (except the highest). Flocks often seen on roads, near cattle ponds, at feeding stations and chicken farms.

Habits   Eats a variety of grain and seeds, also nibbles *Hibiscus* leaves. Nests year-round, but chiefly Mar–Jul, in covered situations, e.g. holes in trees, at the base of Palm fronds, in Cypress trees, eaves of houses etc.

Range   South America. Introduced into the Hawaiian Islands, Panama, Puerto Rico and Jamaica. A few pairs are said to have been released at the Rectory in Black River in the 1820s, and the species is now well-established island-wide.

Plate 69   Saffron Finch – immature

Plate 70   Saffron Finch – adult

BLACKBIRDS AND ORIOLES (ICTERINAE)

A Western Hemisphere subfamily not related to the Oriolidae of the Old World. Most have sharply pointed conical bills for probing under bark, into seed pods or into the ground. The Jamaican Blackbird *(Nesopsar nigerrimus)* is an endemic genus, while the other two residents are endemic subspecies.

Bobolink *(Dolichonyx oryzivorus)*
OCTOBER PINK, BUTTER BIRD, RICE BIRD   15 cm (6 in)

Regular transient Sep–Oct and Mar–May, staying about two weeks. Flocks are usually seen on golf courses, in marshy reeds, vegetable patches, rice-fields and grasslands. In fall they could be mistaken for sparrows as they are in non-breeding plumage.

Voice   They occasionally sing a loud chorus in spring reminiscent of parrotlets but with many bell-like notes, but in the fall they merely 'pink'.

Range   North America, wintering in South America via the West Indies.

Jamaican Blackbird *(Nesopsar nigerrimus)*

WILDPINE SARGEANT, BLACK BANANA BIRD   18 cm (7 in)   Plate 71

Status   Rare resident.

Identification   A shiny black bird with a sharp, pointed black bill, and short, slightly forked rounded tail. Eye dark brown. Legs black. Looks and behaves like a black oriole.

Voice   A loud wheezy 'zwheezoo-whezoo whe'. Call note 'check'.

Habitat   Mature rain forest in the mountains, Newcastle, Worthy Park, Kew Park, Cockpit Country and John Crow Mountains. Most easily seen in the breeding season (May–Jul), at edges of the natural forest between Newcastle and the coffee plantations beyond Hardwar Gap.

Habits   Arboreal. Not found in flocks, unlike other blackbirds. Forages silently in bromeliads and moss or at the base of Tree Fern fronds for insects, tossing out dead leaves and sticks. The rain of debris often first attracts attention to the whereabouts of the bird. Allows close approach when feeding. Nest is cup-shaped, made of dried roots and epiphytes.

Range   Jamaica. An endemic genus and species.

Plate 71   Jamaican Blackbird

Greater Antillean Grackle *(Quiscalus niger))*
CLING-CLING   25.5 cm (10 in)   Plate 72

Status Very common resident.

Identification Glossy black bird with long V-shaped tail, sharply
pointed black bill, and pale yellow eyes. *Female* is slightly smaller and the
V-shaped tail is not as deep. *Immature* has light brown eyes.

Voice Call note sounds like local name, 'cling, cling, cling', but also has
a variety of bell-like notes.

Habitat Cow pastures, cultivated land and around human habitations
especially where they are fed.

Habits Very bold and fearless, often walking around among people.
Roost in large noisy flocks in trees near the sea or on buildings. Nests
(Apr–Jun) in colonies in tall trees, the cup-shaped nest wedged between
the trunk and the branches.

Range Jamaica. *Q.n.crassinostris* is an endemic subspecies. Other subspecies are found in Cuba and the Cayman Islands; Hispaniola and
adjacent islands.

Plate 72   Greater Antillean Grackle

Jamaican Oriole *(Icterus leucopteryx)*

AUNTIE KATIE, BANANA KATIE   20.5 cm (8 in)   Plates 73 & 74

Status   Common resident.

Identification   A greeny-yellow bird with black face and 'bib' on breast. Bill black and sharply pointed with base of lower mandible silver. Wings and tail black margined white, and a large white patch in wings. *Immatures* have cinnamon tips to wing coverts forming two wing bars, and cinnamon spotting on head and back. Lower eyelid salmon. Tail greenish-yellow.

Voice   'You cheat, you cheat', sometimes 'cheat-you'. Song (Oct–Jun) a melodious 'Auntie Atie'.

Habitat   Common in gardens and forests at all elevations.

Habits   Nest (Mar–Aug) an open-work crocheted hanging nest of dried *Tillandsia*, grass stalks or even plastic threads, depending on material available. Feeds on insects which it extracts from pods (e.g. *Poincianna*) and from under bark and in bromeliads by inserting closed beak and prising them open. Also eats fruit and flowers.

Range   Jamaica. The endemic subspecies *I.l.leucoteryx* is the largest of the race. Also found in St Andrew's Island. Extirpated from the Cayman Islands.

Plate 73   Jamaican Oriole – immature

Plate 74   Jamaican Oriole – adult

Northern Oriole *(Icterus galbula)*
Baltimore Oriole   18 cm (7 in)

Uncommon but regular winter transient (Oct–Nov and Jan–Apr), a few spend the winter in lowland and mountain gardens and orchards. Eats Ackee, Privet, *Erythrina.*

Range North America, wintering via Central America and Greater Antilles to South America.

Weavers (Ploceidae)

A tropical African family, often fancied as caged birds.

Yellow-Crowned Bishop *(Euplectes afer)*
GOLDEN BISHOP, NAPOLEON BISHOP   14 cm (5.5 in)

Status   Many individuals escaped from a pet-shop cage during hurricane Gilbert on 12 September 1988 and are now established on Caymanas pond.

Identification   Entire upperparts and breast bright yellow, with some brownish streaking on hind neck. Lower face, neck and upper breast as well as centre of abdomen jet black. Wings brown, short and rounded. Tail dark brown, short with yellow tail coverts extending almost to tip of tail. Legs pinkish. Females and non-breeding males are sparrowlike.

Voice   A high-pitched squeaky song, reminiscent of the Vervain hummingbird.

Habits   Perches on dead trees in the water, returning repeatedly to the same area after short, fluttery flights into the reeds. Feeds on insects and seeds.

Habitat   Marshy areas. In other countries also found in cultivated areas, usually near water.

Range   Central Africa. Introduced and established in Puerto Rico.

Appendix 1

List of vagrants and rare transients

(Seen less than three times in the last 25 years)

Red-footed Booby *(Sula sula)*
American White Pelican *(Pelecanus erythrorhynchos)*
Double-crested Cormorant *(Phalacrocorax auritus)*
Roseate Spoonbill *(Ajaja ajaja)*
Fulvous Whistling Duck *(Dendrocygna bicolor)*
Northern Pintail *(Anas acuta)*
Cinnamon Teal *(Anas cyanoptera)*
Canvasback *(Aythya valisineria)*
Redhead *(Aythya americana)*
Bufflehead *(Bucephala albeola)*
Sharp-shinned Hawk *(Accipiter striatus)*
Broad-winged Hawk *(Buteo platypterus)*
Piping Plover *(Charadrius melodus)*
Lesser Golden Plover *(Pluvialis dominica)*
Snowy Plover *(Charadrius alexandrinus)*
American Oystercatcher *(Haematopus palliatus)*
American Avocet *(Recurvirostra americana)*
Marbled Godwit *(Limosa fedoa)*
Wilson's Phalarope *(Phalaropus tricolor)*
Herring Gull *(Larus argentatus)*
Common Tern *(Sterna hirundo)*
Parasitic Jaeger *(Stercorarius parasiticus)*
Scaly-naped Pigeon *Columba squamosa*

Black-billed Cuckoo *(Coccyzus erythropthalmus)*
Chimney Swift *(Chaetura pelagica)*
Eastern Wood-Pewee *(Contopus virens)*
American Robin *(Turdus migratorius)*
Solitary Vireo *(Vireo solitarius)*
Yellow-throated Vireo *(Vireo flavifrons)*
Blue-winged Warbler *(Vermivora pinus)*
Golden-winged Warbler *(Vermivora chrysoptera)*
Nashville Warbler *(Vermivora ruficapilla)*
Blackpoll Warbler *(Dendroica striata)*
Cerulean Warbler *(Dendroica cerulea)*
Kentucky Warbler *(Oporornis formosus)*
Mourning Warbler *(Oporornis philadelphia)*
Hooded Warbler *(Wilsonia citrina)*
Wilson's Warbler *(Wilsonia pusilla)*
Canada Warbler *(Wilsonia canadensis)*
Blue Grosbeak *(Guiraca caerulea)*
Painted Bunting *(Passerina ciris)*
Dickcissel *(Spiza americana)*
White-crowned Sparrow *(Zonotrichia leucophrys)*
White-winged Crossbill *(Loxia leucoptera)*

Scientific names of plants mentioned in the text

Common names	Scientific names
Ackee	*Blighia sapida*
Bamboo	*Bambusa vulgaris*
Bitterwood	*Picrasma excelsa*
Blue Mahoe	*Hibiscus elatus*
Bougainvillea	*Bougainvillea* spp.
Broadleaf	*Terminalia latifolia*
Bromeliads	*Tillandsia* spp., *Hohenbergia* spp., *Guzmania* spp.
Broughtonia	*Broughtonia sanguinea*
Bullet	*Bumelia* spp.
Burnwood	*Metopium brownii*
Cashaw	*Prosopis juliflora*
Casuarina	*Casuarina equisetifolia*
Chinese Hat	*Holmskioldia sanguinea*
Cho-cho	*Sechium edule*
Coconut	*Cocos nucifera*
Coffee	*Coffea* spp.
Erythrina	*Erythrina* spp.
Fiddlewood	*Citharexylum caudatum*
French Peanut	*Sterculia apetala*
Ganja	*Cannabis sativa*
Ginger Lilies	*Hedychium* spp.
Guava	*Psidium guava*
Guinea Grass	*Panicum maximum*
Hibiscus	*Hibiscus rosa-sinensis* var.
Indian Corn	*Zea mays*
Jamaican Mistletoe	*Loranthaceae* spp.
Logwood	*Haematoxylum campechianum*
Mangrove (Black)	*Avicenna germinans*
(Button)	*Conocarpus erectus*
(Red)	*Rhizophora mangle*
(White)	*Laguncularia racemosa*
Maiden Plum (Poison Sumac)	*Comocladia* spp.
Maypole	*Agave sobolifera*

Mountain Pride	*Spathelia sorbifolia*
Naseberry	*Manilkara zapota*
Oncidium	*Oncidium tetrapetalum*
Orange	*Citrus* spp.
Peach	*Prunus persica*
Pentas	*Pentas* spp. (Rubiaceae)
Peppers	*Capsicum* spp.
Pimento	*Pimenta dioica*
Pine trees	*Pinus caribaea*
Plantain	*Musa* spp.
Poincianna	*Delonix regia*
Prickly Pear	*Opuntia dillenii*
Prickly Yellow	*Fagara martinicensis*
Privet	*Pithecellobium unguis-cati*
Pudding Withe	*Cissus sicyoides*
Red Birch	*Bursera simaruba*
Royal Palm	*Roystonea* spp.
Santa Maria	*Calophyllum calaba*
Soursop	*Annona muricata*
Spanish Moss	*Tillandsia usneoides*
Spanish Needle	*Bidens pilosa* var. *radiata*
Spathodea	*Spathodea campanulata*
Strangler Fig	*Ficus* spp.
Sweetwoods	*Nectandra* spp.
Tamarind	*Tamarindus indica*
Thatch Palms	*Calyptronoma* spp., *Sabal* spp., *Thrinax* spp., *Coccothrinax* spp.
Tree Ferns	*Cyathea* spp.
Trumpet Tree	*Cecropia peltata*
Vervain	*Stachytarpheta jamaicensis*
Vines (dry limestone forest)	Asclepiadaceae
Waxwood	*Myrica cerifera*
West Indian Cedar	*Cedrela odorata*
Wild Bauhinia (Bullhoof)	*Bauhinia divaricata*
Winterberry	*Ilex macfadyenii*
Yacca	*Podocarpus urbanii*

Appendix 3

Information for visiting bird watchers

Clothing

Lightweight, light-coloured trousers and long-sleeved shirts are the best attire for bird watchers. A hat is essential. A light jacket or sweater will be needed in the mountains because early mornings and foggy afternoons can be chilly and damp. Tucking trousers into long waterboots (Wellingtons) or socks is one of the best ways to reduce the risk of being attacked by ticks when birding in pastures or other areas frequented by cattle (see below). It can be showery at almost any time of the year. A light waterproof bag or day pack will help to protect binoculars, cameras and books.

Electricity

Most parts of Jamaica have mains electricity. The supply is 110 V and 50 cycles.

Transportation

If planning to tour the island to see birds it is essential to have a vehicle at your disposal. Cars, four-wheel drive vehicles and buses can be rented. During the high season (mid-December to April) rental cars are in great demand and it is advisable to book in advance. Cars are driven on the left. The public transportation system (buses and vans) is not recommended for birders. Taxis can be very expensive when hired from tourist centres.

Food and water

All public water supplies are treated and tap water is safe to drink. There are small eating places and restaurants throughout Jamaica.

Pests

Jamaica has no poisonous snakes and very few dangerous insects. There are no chiggers. Mosquitoes and sandflies pick on newcomers. They tend to bite at dawn and dusk; repellent applied at these times will reduce suffering. Sandflies are a problem at dawn and dusk on some (but not all) beaches. Ticks are common in pastures and paths used by cattle. The smallest are less than the size of a pin-head. Tucking long trousers into long boots; avoiding sitting down in pastures; and constantly checking for signs of ticks on clothes are ways to reduce chances of a serious attack. If found, they should be brushed off immediately, and infested clothing should be changed and not worn again until they have been washed. For visits to prime tick country (e.g. Cockpit Country) during tick season (January to March) a spare pair of trousers could be carried so one can change if necessary. The best way to get ticks off one's body is to ask a friend to remove them with a pair of tweezers!

On remote south coast beaches there is a small chance of disturbing basking crocodiles. In normal circumstances crocodiles will go to great lengths to avoid people but one should be aware of their presence as females guarding their nests could be dangerous.

There are several trees and creepers which can cause allergic reactions similar to Poison Ivy. The worst, Maiden Plum (also known as Poison Sumac), is common in limestone forests. For some people contact with any part of the tree causes serious blistering. The sap is the most potent part. Several vines and herbaceous plants are collectively known as cow itch. Their effects are irritating but temporary. The irritants of some types of cow itch are carried on small hairs. Rubbing dry earth on the affected area will quickly relieve the irritation. It is wise to avoid contact with these plants by keeping to paths and tracks.

Appendix 4

Care of injured or orphaned birds

Great care must be exercised before removing birds from the wild, even when they appear to be injured or abandoned. A young bird may crash land on its first flight, then rest, immobile, on the ground apparently unable to move. At this stage it is still being cared for by its parents who will be reluctant to come to it if people are nearby. It is better to leave a bird alone or simply remove it from immediate danger by placing it in a nearby tree or shrub. The parents will then be attracted to its cries and will soon find it.

Occasionally a bird is obviously injured and in need of a short period of protection. It should be placed in a large cage or box in a shady, quiet place, out of the reach of cats and dogs. Clean water must be provided. The bird should be handled as little as possible. Some idea of the type of food which should be provided can be obtained from this book.

Few wild birds (especially insectivores) survive well in captivity. They should be released as quickly as possible. If a bird dies, or if freshly dead specimens are found, their bodies should be wrapped in newspaper and put in a plastic bag in the freezing compartment of the refrigerator and then should be offered to the Institute of Jamaica, Natural History Division, as they may find it useful for their collections.

Glossary

Endemic species   Species whose ranges are restricted to Jamaica.

Subspecies   Members of geographically separated species, which differ in plumage, voice or behaviour from populations in other areas, but which interbreed if and when their ranges meet.

Gape   Opening between mandibles.

Introduced   Species that were introduced to Jamaica and now breed in the wild.

Margined   The edge of the structure described is completely surrounded by a given colour.

Orbital skin   Unfeathered eye ring.

Resident species   Species which are indigenous to Jamaica, breed in Jamaica and which are present throughout the year.

Summer resident species   Species breeding in Jamaica in the summer but migrating in winter.

Tipped   The posterior edge is a certain colour.

Transient   Species regularly migrating through Jamaica. Some species might be rare winter residents.

Vagrant   Species occurring very rarely or accidentally (e.g. as the result of unusual weather conditions). Some species might be very rare transients or winter visitors. For the purposes of this book a bird was considered a vagrant if it had been reliably reported fewer than three times in the last 25 years.

Winter resident species   Species breeding in Jamaica in winter but migrating in summer.

Winter visitor   Migrant species that spend the winter (or sometimes most of the year) but do not breed in Jamaica.

Bibliography

Adams, C.D. (1971) *The Blue Mahoe and other bush, an introduction to plant life in Jamaica.* Sangster's Book Stores Ltd., Kingston, Jamaica.

Adams, C.D. (1972) *Flowering plants of Jamaica.* University of the West Indies, Mona, Jamaica.

American Ornithologists's Union (1983) *Checklist of North American birds.* 6th edition. Allen Press, Lawrence, KS, 877pp.

Asprey, G. & Robbins, R. (1953) 'The vegetation of Jamaica'. *Ecological Monographs,* **23**:359–412.

Bannerman, D.A. (1949) *The Birds of tropical West Africa,* **7**:192

Bond, J. (1936–85) *Birds of the West Indies.* 1st–5th editions. Collins, London.

Bond, J. (1948) 'Origin of bird fauna of the West Indies'. *Wilson Bulletin:* **60**.

Bond, J. (1956) *Checklist of birds of the West Indies,* and 25 supplements, 1956–84. Acad. Nat. Sci. Philadelphia.

Bradley, P.E. (1985) *Birds of the Cayman Islands,* P.E. Bradley, Grand Cayman, B.W.I.

Cory, C.B. (1889) *The birds of the West Indies.* Estes and Lauriat, Boston.

Cruz, Alexander (1972) 'Food and feeding behaviour of the Jamaican Crow, *Corvus jamaicensis.*' *Auk* **89**/2.

Cruz, Alexander (1973) 'Food and foraging ecology of the Chestnut-bellied Cuckoo.' *Wilson Bulletin* **85**/3.

Cruz, Alexander (1976) 'Food and foraging ecology of the American Kestrel in Jamaica.' *Condor* **78**/3.

Cruz, Alexander (1973) 'Food and foraging ecology of the Jamaican Becard.' *Auk* **90**/4.

Cruz, Alexander (1978) 'Adaptive evolution in the Jamaican Blackbird, *Nesopsar nigerrimus.*' *Ornis Scand.* **9**.

FAO/UNEP (1981) *Tropical forest resource assessment project.* FAO UN Technical reports, nos. 1–3. Rome.

Gosse, P.H. (1847) *The birds of Jamaica.* Van Voorst, London.

Gosse, P.H. (1849) *Illustrations of the birds of Jamaica.* Van Voorst. London.

Gosse, P.H. (1851) *A naturalist's sojourn in Jamaica.* Longmans, London.

Gosse Bird Club (1962–88) *Gosse Bird Club broadsheets,* nos. 1–50.

Government of Jamaica (1987) *Jamaica: Country environment profile.* Ministry of Agriculture, NRCD and R.M. Field Associates Inc. Kingston, Jamaica.

Hawkes, A. (1974) *Wildflowers of Jamaica.* Collins/Sangster, London/Kingston.

Haynes, A. (1987) 'Human exploitation of seabirds in Jamaica.' *Biological Conservation* **41**:99–124.

Haynes-Sutton, A. & Sutton, R. (1988) *Conservation of birds in Jamaica, 1988.* Presented to *Themes in Caribbean Ornithology, 1988 Symposium and meeting of the Society for the study of the Caribbean Ornithology,* May 1988, St Croix, US Virgin Islands.

Howard, R. & Moore, A. (1980) *A complete checklist of the birds of the world.* Oxford University Press, England.

Jeffrey-Smith, M. (1956) *Bird-watching in Jamaica.* Pioneer Press, Jamaica.

Johnson, T. (1984) 'Biodiversity and conservation in the Caribbean: profiles of selected islands.' *International Council for Bird Preservation, Monographs, No..1,* ICBP, Cambridge

Lack, D. (1976) *Island biology, illustrated by the land birds of Jamaica.* Vol. 3. Blackwell Scientific Publications, Oxford, UK.

Maltby, E. (1986) *Waterlogged wealth: why waste the world's wet places?* IIED, London and Washington.

National Geographic Society (1983) *Field guide to the birds of North America.* National Geographic Society, Washington D.C.

Peters, J. *et al.* (1931–70) *Checklist of birds of the world.* Harvard University Press, Cambridge, Mass.

Peterson, R. (1980) *A field guide to the birds east of the Rockies.* Houghton Miflin Co., Boston.

Robbins, C., Bruun, B & Zim, H. (1983) *Birds of North America.* Golden Press, NY.

Schuchmann, K. (1980). *Die Jamaika-kolibris,* Trochilus polytmus *und* Trochilus scitulus. Biotropic-Verlag, Frankfurst and Main, W. Germany.

Senior, Olive (1983) *A–Z of Jamaican heritage.* Heinemann Educational Books (Caribbean) Ltd.

Smith, F. (1982) *Naturalist's color guide.* American Museum of Natural History, Washington.

Stewart, D. (ed.) (1984) *Gosse's Jamaica 1844–45.* Institute of Jamaica Publications, Kingston, Jamaica.

Sutton, R. (1987) *Ornithological Survey of the Negril Royal Palm Forest.* Unpublished report to the Petroleum Corporation of Jamaica.

Svensson, S. (1983) *Ornithological Survey of the Negril and Black River Morasses, Jamaica.* Petroleum Corporation of Jamaica, Kingston.

Taylor, L. (1955) *An introduction to the birds of Jamaica.* Macmillan, London.

Terres, J. (1980) *The Audubon Society Encyclopedia of North American birds.* Knopf, New York.

Thompson, D.A., Bretting, P.K. & Marjorie Humphreys (eds.) (1986) *Forests of Jamaica,* papers from the Caribbean Regional Seminar on forests of Jamaica held in Kingston, Jamaica 1983. Jamaican Society of Scientists and Technologists.

Index